NETWORKING
WITH THE
IBM®
TOKEN-RING

NETWORKING
WITH THE
IBM®
TOKEN-RING

CARL TOWNSEND

TAB BOOKS Inc.
Blue Ridge Summit, PA 17214

FIRST EDITION
FIRST PRINTING

Library of Congress Cataloging in Publication Data

Townsend, Carl, 1938-
Networking with the IBM Token-Ring.

Includes index.
1. IBM Token-Ring Network (Local area network system)   I. Title.
TK5105.8.I24T68   1987   004.6′8   87-10096
ISBN 0-8306-2892-4 (pbk.)

Questions regarding the content of this book
should be addressed to:

Reader Inquiry Branch
Editorial Department
TAB BOOKS Inc.
P.O. Box 40
Blue Ridge Summit, PA 17214

The top-down authoritarian management style is yielding to a networking style of management, where people learn from one another horizontally, where everyone is a resource for everyone else, and where each person gets support and assistance from many different directions.

—John Naisbitt and Patricia Aburdene,
Re-inventing the Corporation

Contents

Acknowledgment   xi

Introduction   xii

1 The Local Area Network   1

What Is a Local Area Network? 2
LAN Advantages and Disadvantages 2
Design Goals for LANs 4
Alternative Approaches to Local Area Networking 5
LAN Applications 7
Purchasing a Local Area Network 10

2 Classifying LANs: Network Structures   11

Network Topologies 11
   The Star Topology—The Bus Topology—The Ring Topology—Alternative Topologies
Physical vs. Logical Topologies 17

3 Classifying LANs: Channel Control and Access   20

Introduction to Communications 20
Channel Access 22
   Contention—Polling and Token Ring—Which Method Is Best?

4 Components of a LAN   26

The Four Configurations 26
The IBM Token-Ring Hardware 27

The Workstation—The Server—The Multistation Access Unit—Cabling
Gateways 30
The IBM Token-Ring Network Software 30

5 LAN Cabling   34

Coaxial Cable 34
Twisted-Pair Cable 35
   Data-Grade Cable—Voice-Grade Cable—Connecting Multistation Access Units
Fiber Optics 39
The Wiring Closet 39

6 Rules and Conventions   40

The Seven Layers 42
   The Application Layer—The Presentation Layer—The Session Layer—The Transport Layer—The
   Network Layer—The Data Link Layer—The Physical Layer
Layer Functions in the IBM Token-Ring Network 45

7 Planning for the LAN   46

What Are the Goals? 46
Defining the Limits 48
Examine Your Priorities 48
Surveying the Need 49
Network Loading 51
Getting the Details 53
   Hardware Resources—Memory Requirements—Software Resources—Cable Planning
The Human Factor 57
   Defining Human Resources—Allocating Users and Servers
Selecting Your Vendor 59

8 Using the Disk Operating System   61

Using Batch Files 61
   The PATH Command—The APPEND Command—The JOIN Command—The SUBST Command—
   The PERMIT Command
The "Lost" Commands 66
Starting DOS 67

9 Installing the Network: Adapter Testing and Cabling   69

The Multistation Access Unit 70
The LAN Adapter Card 70
   Setting the Switches—Installing and Testing the Card—LAN Adapter Troubleshooting
Building a Prototype System 73
Installing the Cable 73
Closets, Wires, Documentation 74

10 Installing the Network: Names and Directories   75

Assigning Names 75
   Session Names—Private Subdirectory Names—Network Names
Installing the PC LAN Software 77
   Installing a Diskette-Based Workstation—Installing a Hard-Disk Workstation—Installing PC LAN on
   a Server
Completing the Installation 86
Adding Non-IBM Application Programs 89
Documenting the Installation 91

11 Starting the PC LAN Program   92

Starting the Network 94

The Menu Alternative—Starting from the Command Line—Automatic Start
Saving the Configuration   100
Using the Menus   103
Stopping the Network   104
Reconfiguration and Startup Parameters   104

12 Starting the Server: Sharing Resources   106

Sharing Directory Resources   107
   Using the Menu—Using the NET SHARE Command—Automatic Sharing
Printer Allocation   113
   Using the Menu—Using the Command Line—Automating Printer Sharing
Using Passwords   115
Withdrawing Offers to Share   116
Using Startup Parameters   118
Documenting Your Work   118
Saving Configurations   119

13 Using Resources: The Workstation   120

Directory Resources   120
   Using the Menu—The NET USE Command—Automatic Use Requests
Printer Resources   124
   Using the Menu—Using the Command Form—Using the Automatic Form
Withdrawing Offers to Use   128
   Using the Main Menu—Withdrawing with NET USE
Startup Parameters that Control Sharing   129
Saving and Printing the Configuration   130

14 Sending and Receiving Messages   131

The Message System   131
   The Log File—Using the Buffer—Immediate Viewing
Sending Messages   133
   The Command Mode—The Menu Mode
Receiving Messages   136
   Using a Log File—Using Buffers
Using Additional Names   142
   Defining Aliases with a Command—Defining Aliases with the Menu
Forwarding Messages   143

15 Special Networking Commands   147

Suspending Network Operation   147
   Disk Redirection (DRDR)—Print Redirection (PRDR)—The Print Background Program (PRT)—
   Message Reception (RCV or MSG)—Server Activity (SRV)
Starting and Terminating Suspensions   151
Creating Temporary Servers   153
   Advantages and Disadvantages—Making an Offer with PERMIT—Taking Up the Offer—Terminating

16 Managing Network Printers   158

Initializing and Startup Parameters   160
   REQ: Server Requests—RQB: Network Transmission Buffer Size—TSI: Server Time Allocation—
   PRB: Print Buffer—PCx: Print Count
Managing the Print Queue   162
Using NET PAUSE   164
Forcing Printing   165
The Separator Page   165
Printer Recovery   168

17 Managing the Local Area Network   170

Human Resources   170

The Administrator—The System Integrator—The Server Operator—The Users
Backing Up Network Files   172
Preventive Maintenance   173
Batch Files Revisited   174
   The Startup Batch Files—Other Batch Files
Security   177
Using Application Programs   178

18 Alternative Networks   181

The 3Com Token Plus Network   182
Novell's Netware   182
The IBM PC Network   184

Appendix A: Controlling Network Performance   187

Appendix B: *PC LAN* Command Overview   193

Appendix C: Application Software   197

Glossary   199

Index   202

Acknowledgment

I wish to express my grateful appreciation to Janet Johnson, Charles Boyce, and Charlie Appleby of Pac Tel for their help and technical support.

Introduction

DURING THE SIXTIES AND SEVENTIES A GROWING NUMBER OF COMPANIES discovered that computers were essential for information management in business. The computers of those times were large, expensive systems that required a considerable amount of technical expertise to manage and use effectively.

Today the computing power in corporations is more distributed, often entirely in the hands of the user. Computer programs require far less technical expertise to use, and a small desktop system may have the computing power of a mainframe system of a few years ago. The cost of computing power has dropped so that even the smallest business can afford computers to manage their information. The mainframe computer is still important, but it now handles problems that were beyond the scope of any computer a few years ago.

As companies wrestled with the concept of distributed computing power, a common problem began to emerge. Data and information used to make decisions was often distributed among two or more computers. Files could be moved between computers on diskettes, but the real problem went deeper than this. Corporation data frequently changed to reflect the dynamics and life of the organization. Data on a disk is like a snapshot, representing a picture of something in the company at a particular time. Some type of hardware and software to bring the power of the distributed computers together, creating a dynamic entity that reflected the changing nature of the corporation was, needed. It was from this concern that the idea of networking was born.

In a networking system distributed computers and their users are connected. They can communicate with each other, sharing data and expensive resources as a common community. There is synergy, and the whole is more than the sum of the parts.

This Book

This book is about networking. It is about the local area network, a particular type of network. In a local area network (LAN), computers in close geographic proximity are connected to enable the users to communicate with each other and share resources. This book is concerned with a particular type of LAN, the IBM Token-Ring Network.

The IBM Token-Ring Network was announced in 1986 by IBM and immediately became the standard that others sought to emulate. Token ring hardware was completely new, providing much better throughput under heavy loads than the older PC Network hardware. The software was a revision of the older *PC Network Program*. The new *PC Local Area Network Program* (which I'll call *PC LAN* for the remainder of this book) now functions on either the new token ring hardware or the older PC Network hardware.

For the first time, personal computer users had a viable standard that could meet the demanding needs of the rapidly growing networking requirements of the corporate world. The Token-Ring Network was simple to install and use, worked with the majority of IBM-compatible systems, required only minor modifications of application software, could handle large load factors, and had the potential to become very inexpensive.

This book does not require you to become a computer expert. It is specifically designed for network managers, users, and operators—anyone who has to use a network to accomplish production goals. Technical terms are minimized and, when used, are carefully defined. The emphasis is on planning, installing, and using the network—not on how it works.

How the Book Is Organized

This book is organized in two parts. The first six chapters are tutorial. You will learn some basics about local area networking and some of the network terminology. The second part describes the installation and use of the IBM Token-Ring Network hardware and software.

If you have had some network experience, you should still scan the first part, as it describes some basic information specific to the IBM Token-Ring Network.

The first part contains six chapters. Chapter 1 introduces you to the LAN. You will learn what a ring is. The second chapter describes how LANs can be classified by structure or topology. Chapter 3 describes other ways of classifying LANs, such as by the way they control the channel or the way they access the channel. You will learn what a token means in this chapter. The fourth chapter defines the various parts of the IBM Token-Ring hardware, and the fifth chapter describes network cabling. In the sixth chapter you will find a description of the rules and conventions that are a part of a network system.

The second part describes the planning and installation of the network—how to start it, as well as how to use it. It is specific to the IBM Token-Ring Network hardware and *PC LAN* software. Chapter 7 will help you plan for the LAN. In Chapter 8 you will learn specific DOS features that are a part of the network operation. Chapters 9 and 10 will take you through the installation of the network. In Chapter 11, you will learn how to start the network. Chapter 12 describes how the server shares resources. Chapter 13 describes how the workstations use the resources that are shared. Chapter 14 is an overview of the *PC LAN* messaging system. Chapter 15 will introduce you to special network commands, such as NET PAUSE and PERMIT. In Chapter 16, printer management is described. Chapter 17 is a general overview of network management. Finally, in Chapter 18, you will see how the IBM Token-Ring Network compares with other networks.

Appendices

Four appendices are provided. Appendix A describes how to tune the network for maximum performance. Appendix B is an overview of the network commands. Appendix C is a summary of the popular networking application software that is currently available. Finally, there is a glossary where you can quickly find the meaning of any technical term used in the book.

Chapter 1

The Local Area Network

THE CORPORATIONS AND ORGANIZATIONS ON THE EDGE OF THE FUTURE are discovering that a remarkable change is taking place in our concept of work. Because we are moving rapidly into an information-oriented society, the way we do our work is changing to reflect this new orientation. About 60 percent of us now hold information-management jobs, and this percentage is rapidly increasing.

To support this change, the old bureaucratic structures of the past are giving away to more natural arrangements. The pyramidal and hierarchical organization patterns of past decades are giving way to new patterns that facilitate communication in the new information society—networks, lattices, circles, hubs, and wheels.

As our organizational structures change, it is only natural to expect changes in the information management tools that support our organizations. The large, centralized computer systems of the sixties and seventies were designed to support the hierarchical structures of the organizations that used them. These tools were almost always separated from those who used the information they provided by a priesthood of programmers and data processing managers.

Today, information management systems are increasingly being placed in the hands of those who are using them to make decisions. The manager without a small computer on his or her desk is unusual. As this hardware and software moves directly into the hands of the users, both the hardware and software are changing to support the new concept of networking. These information management systems are taking on the form of the structure of

1

the organizations and networks they support. Communications software, modems, and local area networks are quickly becoming an integral part of today's organizations. This book is about one particular type of networking tool—the IBM Token-Ring local area network.

WHAT IS A LOCAL AREA NETWORK?

For the purpose of this book, a *local area network* (LAN) is a collection of computers linked so they can exchange information and share resources. The networked computers can share printers, data files, programs, and access to minicomputers or mainframe computers at a remote location. "Local Area" implies that the link is within a limited geographic area, normally within the same building.

LAN ADVANTAGES AND DISADVANTAGES

There is a clear need for the local area network in most organizations. Businesses are discovering that 80 percent of their communications requirements occur across relatively short distances, such as within a group of offices or a building.

Here are some of the primary advantages of a LAN:

- Expensive peripherals can be shared by all users. For example: Sue needs a laser printer for only a small part of the day. If the laser printer were part of a network, each person on the network could share the use of Sue's printer.

- Data files can be shared between users. If the Receiving Department and Shipping Department are both updating the inventory file, networking the departments would permit users in both departments to share the same files. Each department would be working with a single file that dynamically reflected the current inventory status.

- Networks can grow incrementally and dynamically to reflect the needs of the organization. Computers can be moved from desk to desk and resources located where the users are located. Alternative systems (such as a single minicomputer) tend to lock the user into a fixed system that has less flexibility. The network is organic, changing as the needs of the users change.

- Managers have instant access to important data primarily used by other managers. For example, a spreadsheet file used by a departmental manager can be easily incorporated into a company spreadsheet by a financial vice-president using the same network.

- Security methods can be implemented to control access to programs and files.

- Network users can share access to larger computers and public access networks.

- Specialized system functions (graphics, communications, etc.) can be implemented on a single system and the function shared by several users.

- Today's personal computers provide a cost-effective method of automating internal communications. Networks generally include some type of message system to support communications between users. A manager can access the network, leave a message for a departmental meeting at eleven, then leave for a 10 A.M. meeting with other managers.

In a local area network data can be transferred quickly between key people who are making decisions. The LAN adds synergy to the network of users—the whole is more than the sum of the parts (see Table 1-1).

There are also some disadvantages of local area networking. Unless there is a clear need to share data quickly, it is often better to move the data on disks between the systems.

- The financial cost of local area networking is still high in comparison with many other alternatives. If Sue plans to use a network to share a laser printer, she might find it cheaper to purchase another laser printer than to purchase today's networking hardware and software.

- Local area networking software requires memory space in each of the computers used on the network. For an IBM PC/XT 640K

Table 1-1. The Local Area Network Versus the Single-user System.

ADVANTAGES	DISADVANTAGES

Economic
   Shared peripherals (as printers)
   Technological flexibility
   Incremental growth
Organizational
   Improved communications
   Improved standardization
   Better control
   Controlled security
   Data sharing
	Less computer memory available
	High cost
	Higher complexity
	Less user control
	Ease of security loss

computer in an IBM Token-Ring Network that has a printer or disk space shared with other users, almost 50 percent of the computer's memory will be needed to manage the network interface. This reduces the memory space available for the user's programs.

- Local area networking adds another level of complexity to the computer operation. Users may have difficulty learning the network commands. The installation and management of a LAN requires far more technical and administrative skills than installing and managing several computers that are not networked.

- Some control on the part of the user is lost. You may have to share a printer with other users, or discover that the entire network suddenly locks up because one user makes a mistake.

- Some type of security system must be implemented if it is important to protect private data.

- Many current application programs will not run in a network environment. The program may require too much memory or have other technical constraints. In other cases the program may run, but the execution leaves too little memory for data. Memory-intensive programs, such as spreadsheets and expert systems, are particularly vulnerable.

There is no doubt, however, that local area networking is the edge of technology for those working with information management. New computers will have more memory and will be faster, eliminating the problems of the current technology.

DESIGN GOALS FOR LANS

If you plan to install a local area network, there are several design goals that should be considered. In Chapter 7 these will be examined as they apply to the IBM Token-Ring Network. For now we need simply define these as general objectives.

- Low Cost—The price of the personal computer is dropping rapidly, and the price of the adapter card and cables for each system can easily be a significant part of each system's cost. There are also hidden costs (training time, cables, installation labor, and ongoing technical support and management) that may not be obvious in the initial planning.

- Reliability—The network should be reliable. If a user makes a mistake, it should not bring down the whole network. If a computer on the network fails, it should not take the whole network down.

- Speed—The speed of a particular network is an important consideration. The specified bandwidth of the network is not necessarily the primary factor: the actual data throughput is less than this, due to many factors. The bandwidth of the IBM Token-Ring Network is twice that of IBM's older PC Network hardware, yet both have approximately the same throughput. (Chapter 5 explains why this is true.) Other factors are also important, such as the number of users on the system (see Chapter 3).

- Compatibility—You will probably want to connect a wide variety of equipment to your network. You should be sure that the type of network you select will support the equipment you intend to use. The IBM Token-Ring Network, for example, will not currently support a MacIntosh.

- Flexibility and Extendability—You should be sure the network you select will support your long-term goals. Cable requirements, access to mainframe computers, the number of users, or other requirements may limit your choices.

- Simplicity—How hard is it to learn the network commands and to work with the network? How complex is the cabling system? What are the disk format requirements? If the system goes down, how long does it take to restart it?

- Standards—Does the network work with standard disk formats and standard versions of application programs? Does the network system use the MS-NET redirector (more on this in Chapter 6)? If you need special versions of application programs, you will quickly find that you will be unable to use some of the popular software that is already available for many systems. If you have to use special disk formats, this raises questions about the network's adaptability to future DOS releases.

- Security—What provisions for security control does the network provide? Is it easy to bypass the security provisions with a little experience? Are multiple-level security provisions provided?

- Cables—What type of cables does the system use and how easy are they to install?

ALTERNATIVE APPROACHES TO LOCAL AREA NETWORKING

In some cases you may find that alternative network approaches are better than installing a local area network. The five basic alternatives are sneaker networks, the telephone network, alternative long-haul communications, multiprocessing, the I/O bus, and the low-cost zero-slot LAN.

Sneaker networks are the cheapest and most reliable form of networking. All of us network this way, and it requires no hardware or software. Users simply exchange disks and update the files on their computers daily, weekly, monthly, or whenever is necessary. This may work if the files do not need to be simultaneously used during the day by several users.

Telephone networks (or PBX systems) are useful for long-distance (long-haul) communications in which the geographic area to be covered is beyond the range of the local area network. Unfortunately, telephone wiring and switching methods are primarily designed for voice communication. As a result, communication speeds are limited to a fraction of that used in the local area network and the system is largely inefficient for modern data communication.

Telephone networks, however, are a reliable form of networking if high data transfer speeds are not important. All you need is a modem and some communication software. For example, a central corporate location could send messages to salespeople at divisional locations. The telephone network is quite adequate when it only needs to keep up with typing or printing speed.

Alternative long-haul communication services add features to existing telephone networks to provide specialized data communications support. Essentially, they make the voice-based telephone system function as a data network. Typical examples include the Telenet and Tymnet services available in most cities. Such networks have eliminated many of the difficulties of the dial-up telephone access, but network speeds are still limited and are far less than that of a local area network.

Computers contain both parallel and serial ports (*the I/O bus alternative*) that can be used to transfer data directly between systems. A parallel port is the fastest, because with a parallel transfer data is transferred between computers eight bits at a time. Although parallel data transfer is fast, only two computers can be connected at a time and the distance between the systems is limited to about a hundred feet or less. There is no true networking, but this method does permit you to quickly transfer files and messages.

A serial port can only transfer information a bit at a time, and is therefore slower than a parallel port. Systems can, however, be separated by as much as several hundred feet. RS-232C is the standard that is used for serial transfers.

With either a serial or parallel transfer you will want to use special software to manage the transfer, but there is no hardware cost involved except for the cable. The software is relatively inexpensive.

In a *multiprocessor system,* a central computer system is used with multiple processor cards and memory banks in a central system. The user has only a simple video terminal (no local floppy or hard disk) connected to one of the processor cards and a bank of memory. All users share an access to a common hard disk and printer peripherals at the central location. A separate processor card (with memory) is used to manage disk transfers and printing.

This approach offers some of the advantages of a local area network, but is a centralized system on which all the users are dependent. If the central system is down, all the users are down. The users also have less control than with a true network, as the user has no more than a video terminal. There are no storage resources (disks) at the local user terminal.

Zero-slot LANs use a serial port on the computers and software to simulate a local area network. Since the computer processor has to do much of the work and the serial port is a low-speed port, this alternative is quite slow. If your needs consist of simple transfers—perhaps an occasional file to a plotter on a friend's computer, or an occasional message—this low-cost approach at only $100-$200 per computer may be your best alternative.

Upgrading to a larger system has both advantages and disadvantages (see Table 1-2). Using a minicomputer or mainframe computer instead of a LAN puts more control and management in the central location. This may or may not reflect the goals of your organization. If the number of users is small, the larger system has a high cost on a per user basis. As additional users are added, however, the incremental cost may be less than adding users to a LAN (Fig. 1-1). When comparing costs, be sure to include the cost of installation, maintenance and training. If the larger system is an alternative, obtain quotes for upgrading and compare this with purchasing a local area network.

LAN APPLICATIONS

Local area networks can be used wherever it is necessary to share data, programs, or peripherals. In most cases the true reason for the network is to share information, known as *connectivity:* the ability to share information between two or more systems. The systems may be microcomputers, minicomputers, or mainframes. The information is dynamic, changing

Table 1-2. The Multi User System Compared with the LAN.

ADVANTAGES	DISADVANTAGES
• Lower incremental cost if the number of users is large	• Large initial cost if the number of users is small
• Extensive resource available in terms of speed and memory	• Higher complexity—more training required
• Powerful software available, often at less cost than purchasing network software for each user when PCs are used	• Software is expensive and complex
• More adaptable to central control and management	• Technical administration is required
	• Less flexibility

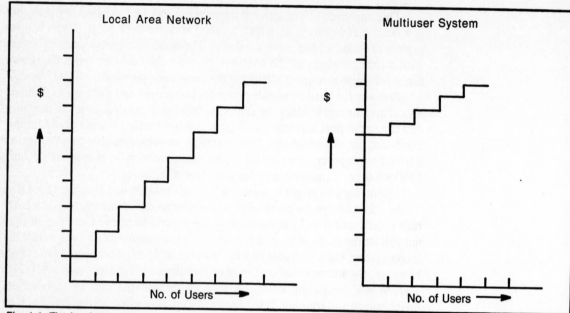

Fig. 1-1. *The local area network and multiuser systems.*

constantly during the day. A LAN is seldom purchased only to enable the users to share a printer or hard disk (although this is plausible).

Whether a network is needed is determined by the application software being used and how it is used. If a database manager is used with files that are updated dynamically by several users, there may be good justification for a LAN. Using the same reasoning, word processing or the creation of spreadsheets may require a LAN if users share common files. It is not very economical to purchase a LAN simply to share a laser printer or to permit the transfer between systems of static files that are updated less than once a day (Fig. 1-2).

Now let's look at some real applications where a local area network is used.

Inventory Control System—Acme Corporation manufactured machine tools and used *dBASE III Plus* to track their inventory. To keep profits at a maximum, it was very important to keep the inventory of parts and completed models as low as possible. Acme had 12 IBM PC-compatible computers located in various departments, all connected with a LAN.

One of the computers contained the master inventory file as well as a bill-of-material file that defined what parts were in what assembly and what assemblies and parts were in each model. The shipping department had their own computer containing their shipping files. Using the network, shipping could as easily access the master files as if they were on a local disk. The sales department had their own computer with their customer files, and could also

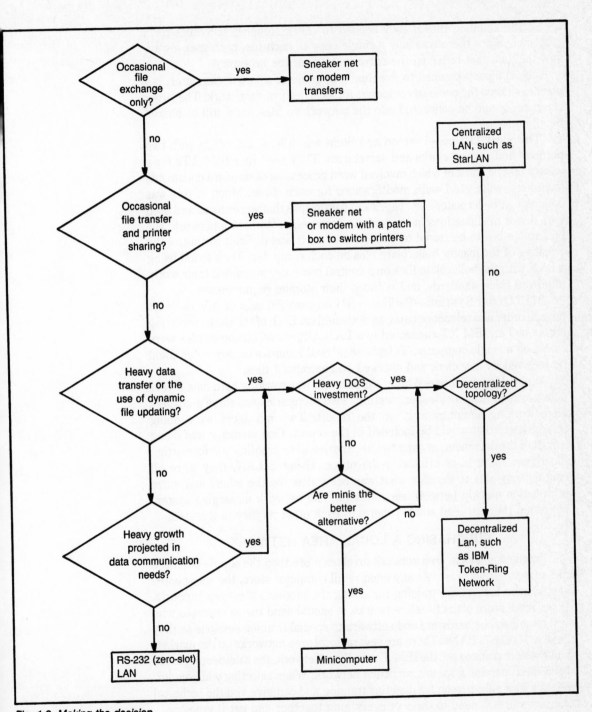

Fig. 1-2. Making the decision.

access the shipping files if they needed to check shipping schedules for a customer. Since there was only a single copy of each file, each user always saw the data that reflected the current status of the inventory.

The company planned to eventually upgrade to a larger computer, but planned to keep the personal computers for local departmental work. The larger computer would be connected into the network so files could still be shared by all departments.

The Law Office—Pearson and Stein was a local law office with two partners and several clerks and secretaries. They used four IBM ATs for a variety of jobs, most of which involved word processing of standard documents (contracts, wills, etc.), with modifications for each client. Much of this was done using "boilerplate," i.e., pages and paragraphs that were stored and used with minor modifications in the various documents. Without a network, the boilerplate had to be stored on each computer. It was difficult to control the updating of the master boilerplate files on each computer. They found using a LAN with the boilerplate files on a central computer simplified their work, improved their standards, and reduced their storage requirements.

Mail Order System—Perkins Seed Company did most of their business by mail order and telephone using an 800 number. Each of the clerks receiving orders had an IBM XT connected to a LAN. Order and customer files were stored on a single computer. Telephone or mail inquiries on any order could be received by any clerk and checked on centralized files.

Word Processing—Widget Corporation was working hard on a 5-year plan for an annual stockholder meeting. Two secretaries and three managers were working simultaneously on the report. Two managers were doing spreadsheets that would be included in the report. One manager was doing a draft of the document, and the two secretaries were proofing and formatting the report for a laser printer in the office. Using a LAN, they were all continuously able to monitor what was being done by the others and move information quickly between each system. The network messaging system permitted them to send status reports to each other as they progressed.

PURCHASING A LOCAL AREA NETWORK

Purchasing a local area network involves more than the simple purchase of hardware or software. At any good retail computer store, the salespeople should have had special training for selling the products the store supports. If the retail store plans to sell networks, it should send the salespeople who will be selling the hardware and software to special training sessions so they have expertise in LANs. There are several local area networks on the market, and if a store plans to sell the IBM Token-Ring Network, the salespeople should have specific training for this particular network. When selecting your vendor, be sure your salesperson has had this training and can give you the technical support you will need to connect everything together and get it going.

Chapter 2

Classifying LANs: Network Structures

IN NETWORK PLANNING, ONE OF THE FIRST DECISIONS THAT MUST BE made is the type of architectural structure desirable for the network. This determines network control and how data is used by the network. This chapter describes the three basic types of network structures, including the structure used by the IBM Token-Ring Network.

NETWORK TOPOLOGIES

A network is composed of nodes and links. A *node* is a connection point in the network for creating, editing, receiving or retransmitting messages. A *link* is a communications path between two nodes. A link can also be called a *channel*. Information passes through the nodes and links, moving from the initiating node to the destination node. In a computer network, computers are located at the nodes and are called *servers* or *workstations*. A workstation is a computer used as a node used primarily to run application programs. A server is a computer that shares its resources with other workstations in the network.

A network *topology* is the geometric arrangement of the links and nodes that make up the network. As the topology of the network is very closely related to how the network is controlled and used, the type of topology chosen for a network should be defined very early in the planning process. Each LAN product has a specific topology. The topology you need is one factor in determining the type of network you need.

One of the first topology decisions to make is whether the network control is to be centralized or decentralized. In a centralized type of control, access to the network (which nodes can use the network and when) and the allocation of the channels (how long a node can use the channel) is controlled from a single node. There is a master/slave relationship between the central computer and the workstations. This permits a high degree of security and centralized control, but also leads to a high level of inertia and lack of flexibility. Once an investment is made in a large, central computer to manage the network (and the related software), it is difficult and expensive to change the network to another system at a later time. A centralized system, however, does provide extensive resources (speed, memory, etc.) for use with complex problems. An engineer can come in at 2:00 A.M. and run the multiuser system as a single-user system with huge dedicated resources.

In a decentralized network, nodes can establish their own connections and access the network independently according to an accepted set of rules. Such a network is more adaptable for control at the user level, but may increase the complexity and cost at the workstation level. Such a system is said to be *peer-to-peer*. The IBM Token-Ring Network is a decentralized network.

Whether a network is to be centralized or decentralized depends upon many factors. These include how the network is to be controlled, the cost of the implementation, the purpose of the network, the number of nodes, the geographic distribution of the nodes and the function of each node. As we shall see, few networks are purely centralized or decentralized. In most companies the actual network topology is often more of a dynamic structure that can include both centralized and decentralized elements.

There are really only three primary network topologies: the star, the ring, and the bus. All other topologies are variations of these basic three.

The Star Topology

The oldest topology used in computer networks is the star. In a star topology all nodes are joined at a central node (Fig. 2-1). All control is from this central node. Any message from a source node to any destination node goes through the central node, where it is routed to the proper destination node. If the destination node is busy, the central node must temporarily store the message until the destination node is available. As a result of the centralized control, the outlying nodes are relieved of any control functions.

The most common example of the star network is the telephone network. There is no direct connection between the nodes, and all message traffic is routed through central branches. The star network is also used in many corporate computer installations of large computer systems. A centralized mainframe or minicomputer is used for most of the primary processing, but users may be able to create, edit and compile programs at local workstations without the need to wait for available processing time on the central computer.

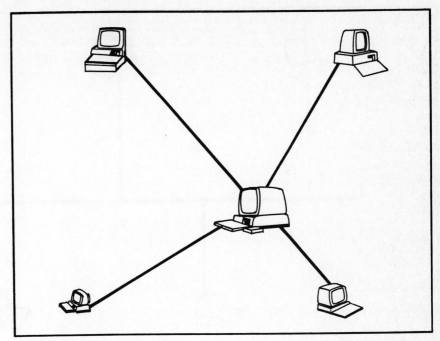

Fig. 2-1. The star topology.

This makes it easy for a data processing manager to control priorities and manage computer resources from the primary computer system, but provides less freedom and control for the individual users. The network is also heavily dependent upon the central computer—if this computer goes down, the entire network is down.

For a corporation with a decentralized type of organizational structure, it may be more appropriate to put more control with the user and depend less upon a central computer. In such an organization the star network would not be appropriate. Because of the star network's dependence upon a single central node, the network is inherently less reliable than other alternatives.

The Bus Topology

In a bus network, a single connecting line, or "bus," is shared by a number of nodes (Fig. 2-2). Each workstation has a unique address. Using the correct address, any workstation can send a message to any other node on the bus. Since there is no host or central node, the network is decentralized, with the network control distributed among the functional nodes.

For example, if Joe wished to send a message or file to Sandy, Joe's workstation would create a data "packet" that would contain the address of Sandy's network workstation with the message. The data packet would then

13

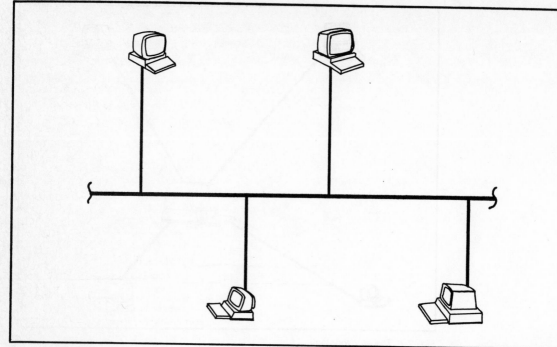

Fig. 2-2. The bus topology.

be transmitted on the common bus. All workstations on the line would receive the message, but only Sandy's station would recognize the message and act on it. Other workstations would ignore the message. Once the message was received, the destination workstation would send an acknowledgement to the source workstation. The bus could then be used for another transmission.

Unlike the star topology, in which messages are transmitted sequentially to specific workstations, in the bus topology messages are broadcast to all workstations. The receiving workstation recognizes its own messages and acknowledges them.

The bus topology is relatively new to the technological scene. It was not economically feasible to put enough intelligence (control) in a local workstation to make the bus topology a viable alternative until the invention of microprocessor chips.

This topology is inherently one of the most reliable topologies—if any node fails, the remainder of the network can continue as usual. The only exception is if a node fails in such a way as to short out the bus, preventing any other node from receiving signals. A second type of failure in the bus system is if a node grabs the bus and fails in such a way that it transmits continuously, preventing other nodes from using the bus. Both of these are rare types of failures.

A third advantage of the bus topology is its low installation cost. Wiring costs are much, much less than for a star network, often only half as much (Fig. 2-3). A single cable connects each local workstation to the next workstation. With the star network, the cable for each workstation must connect to the central system.

Unfortunately, there is a price for decentralized control, lower installation cost, and increased reliability. The complexity required at the local node for the bus topology means that the cost of the local node is higher.

The Ring Topology

The third primary topology is the ring topology. In the ring topology, nodes are connected point-to-point in an unbroken circular configuration that looks like a ring (Fig. 2-4). Like the bus topology, the network is decentralized. Messages are broadcast on the network with an address, and each node only acts on messages specifically addressed to it. There is, however, a distinguishing difference in the ring network. Unlike the bus, each node functions as an active repeater, receiving messages addressed to any node on

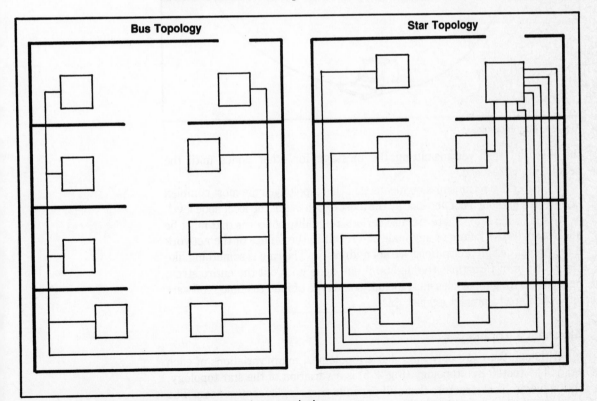

Fig. 2-3. Comparison of wiring costs for bus and star topologies.

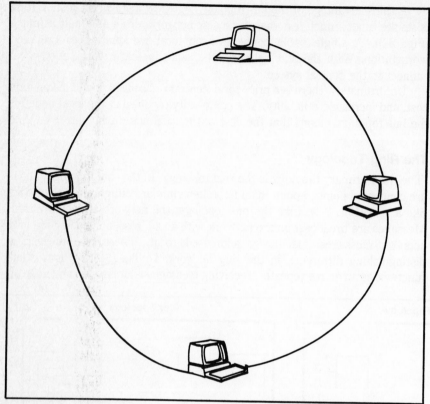

Fig. 2-4. Ring topology.

the link and then retransmitting the message for other nodes until the destination is reached.

The need for retransmission means that this topology is the most complex of the three (although not necessarily the most expensive at the local node level, as we shall soon see). There are also serious reliability concerns that must be addressed, as the failure of any node can result in the failure of the network if the proper design precautions are not addressed. The ring is something like older strings of Christmas tree lights: if one node goes out the entire string may go out. Ring topologies must include some type of fault tolerance software and hardware to protect against this.

Alternative Topologies

Although there are only three basic topologies, many variations of each exist. The rooted tree topology (Fig. 2-5) is a variation of the star topology, with a hierarchical structure that still depends on a single, central node. The major difference in the rooted tree topology from the bus topology is the

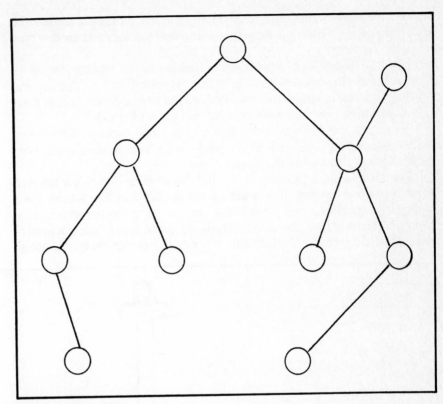

Fig. 2-5. Tree topology.

network's dependence upon at least one critical component located at one of the nodes: a processor, repeater, or other device.

The most common application for the rooted tree topology is the classroom, where a single central computer is controlled by the teacher, but the users still can use their system and resources on the teacher's computer. The student has no access to other classroom systems—only his own, and limited access to the teacher's system. The rooted tree is also used in office buildings where a central computer is used with multiple workstations, often on many floors.

The unrooted tree topology is a variation of the bus topology, with a tree-type bus. As with the bus topology, the failure of a node does not disrupt the network. The older IBM PC Network hardware is an example of an unrooted tree topology.

PHYSICAL VS. LOGICAL TOPOLOGIES

A network may look physically like one type of network and behave like another. The physical topology describes the way the network hardware appears physically, including the way it is wired. The logical topology defines the way the network processes data. As we shall see in the next section, the IBM Token-Ring Network has one type of physical topology and another type of logical topology.

The IBM Token-Ring Network system uses a physical topology that looks like a star and a logical topology like the ring network (Fig. 2-6). The physical topology is a star topology. Individual cables run from a concentration point (MAU or wiring closet) to each user location (or work area).

The logical topology, however, is similar to a ring network. There is no central node and all control is at the workstation level (peer-to-peer). Data circulates in a ring among the workstations.

For this reason the topology of the IBM Token-Ring Network is referred to as a *star-ring topology*. It is wired as a star, but acts like a ring. Each workstation contains a network adapter card that is connected with a cable to a central multistation access unit. The multistation access unit is a passive device that connects the workstations in a ring-like configuration. Although

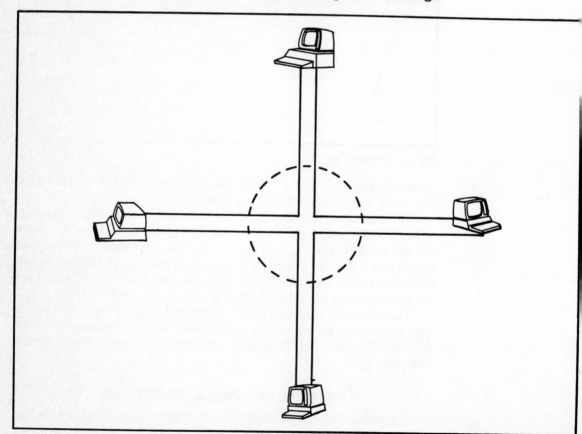

Fig. 2-6. IBM token-ring network topology.

only one physical cable connects to the workstation, it actually must contain two twisted-pair wires. One twisted-pair carries the data from the multistation access unit to the workstation. The second carries the data from the workstation to the multistation access unit. The network adapter card must contain an active repeater, as in any other ring network.

The result is a decentralized topology that functions as a ring topology. IBM included many features to eliminate the reliability problems of the ring network. If a node is disconnected or fails, a relay in the multistation access unit bypasses the unit and enables the network to continue to function. If a cable breaks, the network actually can diagnose where the break occurs and display a message to the user. The primary disadvantage of the star-ring topology is the amount of cable it needs.

Chapter 3

Classifying LANs: Channel Control and Access

A NETWORK CONSISTS OF LINKS AND NODES. THE LINKS ARE THE COM-munication paths between the nodes and are called the channels. In any network, some means must be provided for managing the transfer of data on the channel. The channel is a finite data transfer medium, and its use must be managed efficiently and almost invisibly to the user. This involves two problems that must be resolved: where is channel access controlled, and how is it determined who gets the channel?

The first problem was discussed in the last chapter when we described the two methods of control: centralized and decentralized. In this chapter we will look at the second problem, the question of how the network determines who gets the channel.

INTRODUCTION TO COMMUNICATIONS

Messages can be transmitted over a communications channel in either analog or digital form. Digital signals are discrete, and generally alternate between two states (Fig. 3-1). Almost all modern computers use digital signals for processing. Analog signals, in contrast, are represented by continuous signals that vary in a wave-like pattern (Fig. 3-2). The number of complete cycles per second of an analog signal is said to be its frequency, and this is expressed in hertz. Telephones, television, and radio channels use analog signals.

Any communications channel has a certain *capacity*. This refers to the rate at which the analog or digital signals can be transmitted over the channel. The

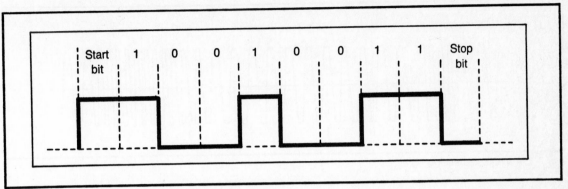

Fig. 3-1. A digital signal.

capacity is measured in terms of the bandwidth of the channel. The greater the channel bandwidth, the greater the capacity of the channel. The IBM Token-Ring Network channel, for example, can support a digital transmission rate of four megabytes a second on the channel.

If a local area network uses analog transmission on the channel, it is said to be a *broadband* network. In a broadband system, the adapter card in each computer must convert the outgoing digital signals to an analog form, and at the same time convert the incoming analog signals to a digital form. Because the channel is analog, however, it can be shared by a number of systems. For example, a company can install a single-cable system that can support a closed-circuit video monitoring system as well as a LAN.

For the analog signal to carry information in a broadband system it must be modulated. The unmodulated signal is called the *carrier*. The carrier is modulated or changed in some way by the digital signal so that it carries the data. In a broadband network, generally either the frequency or the phase of the signal is altered by the digital data (Fig. 3-3). This flexibility has some disadvantages. The adapter cards in each computer have many analog circuit processing components, including the modem. The manufacture and adjustment of the adapters is quite critical, and the components may change with time. The connecting cables must be expensive coaxial cable. IBM's older PC Network hardware uses a broadband system.

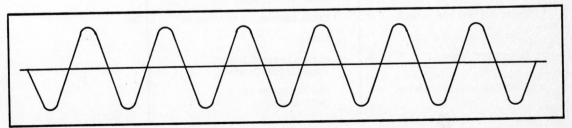

Fig. 3-2. An analog signal.

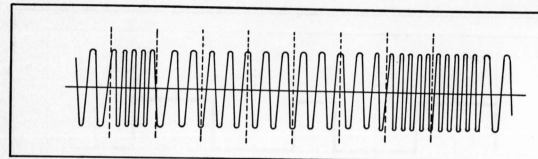

Fig. 3-3. A modulated analog signal.

A *baseband* system, in contrast, puts the digital signal directly on the channel. There is no analog processing, and the adapter card can be reduced to a few chips (although these chips are very complex). The disadvantage is that the channel can only support a single network, and the channel cannot be shared with other systems. Inexpensive twisted-pair cabling can be used if the proper shielding precautions are taken. The IBM Token-Ring Network is a baseband system (see Table 3-1).

CHANNEL ACCESS

Channel access refers to the method the nodes use to gain the use of the channel. Two basic access methods can be used: contention or polling.

Table 3-1. Baseband vs. Broadband Systems.

BASEBAND	BROADBAND
Uses small portion of cable bandwidth	Uses larger portion of cable bandwidth
Passive cable system (no amplifiers)	Active cable system (requires amplifiers in cable)
Stations provide energy for cable transmission	User stations do not provide energy for cable transmission
Cable supports one network	Cable supports many networks
Uses coax or twisted pair	Uses coax
No modem required	Modem required at each station (added expense)
1000 + stations per network	25,000 stations per network or more

Contention

The contention method functions much like a group of people at a cocktail party. If one person wishes to say something and no one else is talking, that person begins to speak immediately. If one wishes to speak and someone else is talking, the person wishing to speak waits until no one is talking. Two people may begin talking at once; if this happens, both stop and wait briefly, then one begins to speak and the other waits.

Contention access is similar to this. One popular method of contention access is called CSMA/CD, an abbreviation of Carrier Sense Multiple Access with Collision Detect. *Carrier sense* indicates that any node must first sense to be sure no one is using the channel before it can begin to transmit. *Multiple access* indicates that several nodes can use the channel. *Collision detect* indicates that if two nodes start transmitting at once and the messages collide, the collision is detected and appropriate steps are taken. Let us look at the process in detail.

If any node wishes to transmit, it first checks to see if a carrier exists on the line. If a carrier exists, this indicates someone else is transmitting and the node waits. If there is no carrier, transmission begins immediately.

Because of delays in the network, there is always a chance that two nodes may sense the empty channel and then begin transmitting simultaneously. If this happens a collision occurs, and the messages will be garbled. Once the collision is detected the nodes stop transmitting. Both nodes wait a random amount of time, then one begins transmitting again. The node detecting the collision normally is designed to put a jamming signal on the channel so that other nodes will know a collision has occurred. Whichever node first begins again gets the channel, and the other waits. The trick here, of course, is to have each node wait a different amount of time. While waiting, it must continue to monitor the channel to be sure it remains unused. While waiting, if another node starts transmitting, the waiting node will lose the channel again.

Once a node starts transmitting, it is in control of the network until it has completed the transmission of its message, then the channel becomes available again.

CSMA/CD is particularly effective if the number of nodes is small and network traffic is low. With larger and busier networks, there is no way to determine how long any particular user will have to wait for network access. Since each node randomly bids for the channel, there is only a statistical probability of the channel being available when it is needed. If a lot of collisions begin to occur, most of the network time is spent waiting, trying to transmit, and failing. Network throughput seriously deteriorates. In practical terms, however, channel access generally works very effectively. CSMA/CD was used by the older IBM PC Network hardware and is still used today by some of 3Com's popular hardware.

Polling and Token Ring

Star networks often use a centralized polling technique to control network access. The host computer determines who has the channel in a predetermined order. The host queries each node in turn, asking if the node has anything to transmit. Access is controlled so that each node has a predetermined time. The time slots can be assigned based on the node network traffic or priority.

If the network is decentralized, there is no host computer and some type of alternative polling method must be devised. The most popular, particularly in the ring and bus topologies, is the token-passing access method. It is this strategy that is used by the IBM Token-Ring Network.

The token ring access method functions much as the old "who's got the button game" you probably played when you were younger. The players stand in a circle with their hands over a string that is tied in a circle. On the circle is a single button or ring that is passed around the circle hidden by the hands. Whoever is "it" tries to guess the location of the object.

In the case of the network, the token is a bit configuration that is passed around the ring. The token can have either of two values: free or busy. When the token value is free it circulates on the ring and the node with the token at a given time is allowed to transmit. The maximum time any node has to wait to transmit is the time for the token to traverse the circle. Even if the network is very busy, no one has to wait more than this predetermined time. The token functions much like a freight train with an empty car. Whoever has the car can change the token to a "busy" token, load the "car" with the source and destination addresses, and then add the message. The resulting package is called a *frame*, and circulates until it reaches the destination node.

The destination node receives the message and adds an acknowledgement, leaving the token set to busy. Once the message has completely circulated the ring and the source node sees the acknowledgement, the source node removes it from the network and changes the token to a free state again. As long as the message is circulating on the ring with the busy token, no other node can transmit.

At any given time, whoever has the token has control of the network. In this sense the control of the network, like in the CSMA/CD method, is decentralized. There are only two basic rules. First, only the node with the token can put a message on the network. Second, only the node that puts the message on the network can remove it. Note: The concept of "message" here is not just an electronic letter for someone on the network. It can be any data that is transferred from one computer to another on the network: part of a word processing file, a portion of a database, or perhaps some of a spreadsheet.

There are two possible failure modes of the token ring method. The first, of course, is the chance that someone will drop the token (the circulating frame with the free token stops circulating). Without a frame with a free token, no

Table 3-2. Comparison of Channel Access Methods.

CONTENTION	TOKEN RING
Commonly used	Growing in popularity
Standard (IEEE 802.3)	Standard (IEEE 802.4)
Distributed control	Distributed control
Excellent performance unless heavily loaded	Best when guaranteed access time is required
Variable access time	Deterministic access time
Distance limitations	Less distance limitations
Many suppliers	Few suppliers

one can use the network. If this happens, no one can transmit. The second is the chance that somehow an extra token gets on the network. The IBM Token-Ring System includes some built-in fault-detection features to elimi-nate these possibilities.

Which Method Is Best?

The CSMA/CD method is best if the network traffic is low and there are only a few nodes. The users are not waiting for the token to come back around the ring.

As the network traffic increases, the number of collisions increases very rapidly. If the network cannot support the traffic, the network appears to lock up and no one can transmit. All the nodes are trying to transmit, sensing a collision, then backing off and waiting.

If the network is busy and there are a lot of nodes, the token-ring method is better, as it assures each node access within a predetermined time. IBM, by choosing the token-ring method, has targeted their planning for large, busy networks which will eventually involve mainframe access (see Table 3-2).

The technology of the token-ring access is basically more complex than the CSMA/CD and requires more "intelligence" on the part of the local node. In using a token-ring baseband system, however, the need for analog components and the resulting adjustments is eliminated. This reduces the adapt-er card in the workstation to a few chips, which should eventually make it possible to put the adapter electronics on the motherboard.

Both methods have been defined with standards to ensure compatibility between manufacturers. The token ring is defined by the IEEE 802.4 stan-dard, and the CSMA/CD contention method by the IEEE 802.3 standard.

Chapter 4

Components of a LAN

A N IBM TOKEN-RING NETWORK CONSISTS OF HARDWARE AND SOFTWARE. The software component is an updated release of the same software developed for the IBM PC Network, now called the *PC Local Area Network Program,* or *PC LAN.* It can be used with either the IBM PC Network hardware or the IBM Token-Ring Network hardware.

From this you might expect to use the IBM Token-Ring Network hardware with other software, or use the IBM *PC LAN* software with other network hardware; this is possible to some extent. Because LAN standards exist, you can mix hardware and software among some vendors. If you plan to do so, however, you should have plenty of technical support and be aware of the advantages and disadvantages in each particular mix. For the purposes of this book I assume the user has the IBM Token-Ring Network, plus the IBM *PC Local Area Network* software.

THE FOUR CONFIGURATIONS

Each computer in a network can be installed to function in any one of four configurations. Each time you start (boot) any computer in the network, you can choose which of the four configurations you wish to assign to it. Each computer is configured separately. The configuration, once assigned, cannot be changed unless you reboot the computer. The four configurations are *redirector, receiver, messenger,* and *server.* Each configuration could be considered part of a hierarchy, with the server supporting the most features and requiring the most memory for the network software. The redirector uses the least memory, but also has the fewest features.

The redirector is the simplest configuration; it permits you to use resources on a network server or to send messages.

The receiver lets you use resources on a server, send and receive messages, and save incoming messages to a log file.

The messenger lets you use resources on a server, send and receive messages, save incoming messages to a log file, forward messages to other workstations, use multiple names to receive incoming messages, and use the network-request key.

The server contains all the features of the messenger, and also permits its own disks, directories, and printers to be shared with other workstations.

Although the server configuration is the most powerful, it is also the most memory-intensive, leaving barely 331K of memory in a 640K system for any applications running at the server workstation. In most cases a basic network would consist of a single server and one or more messenger workstations.

THE IBM TOKEN-RING HARDWARE

The basic hardware components of the IBM Token-Ring Network are:

1. One or more servers. Each server is an IBM-compatible computer with a local area network adapter card installed.

2. One or more workstations with local area adapter cards installed.

3. One or more multistation access units.

4. The connecting cables.

In this chapter we will look in depth at the first three of these items. In the next chapter we will examine the network cables. In larger networks you may wish to use gateways as well, which are connections to other networks and computers.

The Workstation

A *workstation* is a computer used as a node on a network primarily used to run application programs. In the IBM Token-Ring Network, any IBM PC-compatible computer can be used for a workstation. The computer must have some type of disk drive (floppy or hard), used to start the local network software. (In some types of non-IBM LANs, it is not necessary for the workstation to have a disk drive.)

To use these computers as a workstation, you must add the local area network adapter card to the computer, cable the computer into the network, and then add the network software. To use a workstation in the network, the network software must be initiated with the NET START command (see Chapter 10). The workstation must have enough memory to support the network software and the application software.

Note: Some computers marketed as IBM-compatibles will not support the network. Check with a local vendor for network compatibility.

The Server

A *server* is a computer that shares its resources with other workstations in a network. In most systems the primary concern is the sharing of printers and disk resources. In some networks it is possible to share modems (or other communications equipment), access to other networks or computers, and other specialized peripherals.

A *print server* is a computer that shares one or more printers with other workstations on the network. A print server supports multiple users on the network through a process called *print spooling.* As print requests arrive at the print server from the users, the various programs actually "print" to the server's disk, storing each print image as a file in a queue in a disk directory (see Chapter 16). The print server uses a background program (a program that runs in the computer while the machine is also running other, more visible programs) to print each file, in turn, from the print queue. A print server must have a hard disk with sufficient memory to store the maximum number of print requests that may be waiting at a time.

A server that shares disk resources with other computers on the network is said to be either a *disk server* or a *file server.* The distinction between the two is rather technical, but important in terms of the network's capability. A disk server is disk partitioned into volumes, and the volumes are shared with users on the network. Most of the disk interface software is at the local workstation. When a workstation requests data from the server disk, the disk operating system (DOS) on the workstation computes the physical location of the block on the server computer and then requests the block as if it were from a local disk drive.

In personal computer networks, file serving is generally considered more flexible. The IBM Token-Ring Network, as well as the 3Com's newer *3+*, all support the file serving alternative. In a system using a file server, the network software at the workstation intercepts the disk request before DOS can process it. If the request is for data on the server, the entire request is sent to the server, where it is processed. The server sends the required data back to the workstation.

Often a single server may function as both a print and file server, and indeed this is exactly what is done in the IBM Token-Ring Network. You can define any system to be a print server, file server, or both. If you configure a system as a server, it may serve either or both functions.

A server may or may not be used as a workstation at the same time. If a server is used as a server only and not used as a workstation, it is said to be a *dedicated server*. If it is also used as a workstation, it is said to be a *nondedicated server*. In some types of LANs, a dedicated server has no keyboard. The server operator uses peripheral workstations to manage the network (display status, change the print queue, define resources, etc.). In an IBM Token-Ring Network, a 640K server has approximately 331K of memory left that can be used for workstation functions. This is often sufficient to use with some application programs. The user may experience some speed degradation, because the processor must support both network functions and the local application program. In heavily loaded networks, it is generally best not to use the server as a workstation. In some cases you may wish to use multiple servers to manage the network load.

In some networks, such as Novell's *Netware*, the server disk has a special format. The server in an IBM Token-Ring Network has a standard disk format, but often has a special directory configuration (of directories and file organization) specifically designed to support the network.

In this special disk configuration, some of the server disk directories are private and can only be used from the server and an individual workstation; others are public and can be used by any workstation. Programs that are common to all workstations are put in the public directories. For this reason you will wish to create new directories and move programs and data into these directories to support the network more efficiently when you install a network.

In some networks you may have two or more servers. In the IBM Token-Ring Network there is no host or central computer because the network is decentralized. You can define any computer on the network as a server, making its resources available to other computers on the network.

The Multistation Access Unit

The Multistation Access Unit, or MAU, is the hub for any IBM Token-Ring Network. Cables radiate from the MAU to each computer, making a star-like physical configuration. The IBM Token-Ring Network MAU permits up to eight IBM PC-compatible computers or other devices to be connected to the IBM Token-Ring Network.

If there are more than eight computers in the network, multiple MAUs can be used, connected in a ring, effectively forming one large MAU. MAUs can be located at physically separate locations, distributing the hub of the network over a larger distance. If fewer than eight computers are used, you may still wish to use multiple MAUs to cluster the computers at two or more locations (more in Chapter 5).

The MAU is a metal and plastic box about 18 inches long, 4 inches high, and 6 inches deep that has ten data connectors. Eight connectors are used for connecting computers to the network; the other two connectors are used for connecting the MAU to other MAUs. The front panel of the MAU is wider than the body, and the unit is designed for rack mounting or for installation in wiring closets. This is not essential, however, and you can just as easily wall-mount the system near any of the network computers.

The MAU is completely passive and requires no power to operate. Each connector of the MAU is bypassed internally by a relay connection when no computer is connected. When a computer is connected, power from the computer opens an internal relay, permitting the computer to have access to the network. When you disconnect a PC or turn it off, the power to the computer's data connector drops and the relay for that connector removes the computer from the network, preserving the integrity of the network.

Cabling

IBM recommends a special dual twisted-pair cable for connecting the computers to the MAU and connecting the MAUs to each other. This is described in more detail in the next chapter.

GATEWAYS

A *gateway* is an access point at which a network is connected to another network or another computer system. IBM has announced that it plans to introduce gateways to the older PC Network hardware systems and to their larger mainframe systems. Other vendors are expected to announce gateways for the IBM Token-Ring Network to support various systems.

In most cases the gateway hardware consists of an IBM PC-compatible computer, an IBM Token-Ring adapter card, and another adapter card specific to the type of gateway. Special software is used to permit the proper transfer of information.

For example, to connect an IBM Token-Ring Network to a network using the PC Network hardware you would need to create a gateway using an IBM-compatible computer and an adapter card for each network. You would also need the supporting gateway software.

If you wish to connect the network to a mainframe or minicomputer, special gateway software permits the computer to transfer information from one network to or from the large computer. Specific data transfer standards, such as the SNA and SLNC, assure the user that specific gateways will work with equipment from a wide number of vendors.

THE IBM TOKEN-RING NETWORK SOFTWARE

The IBM *PC LAN* is the software component sold by IBM for use with the IBM Token-Ring Network. In addition to DOS 3.2, you will need five components:

- The *PC Local Area Network Program* is the highest level program. It contains the menus, utilities, spooler, and messaging system for the network. As a user, this is the only part with which you are concerned. The use of this program is described in the second part of this book.

- The Redirector is the software that traps requests to a remote disk or printer on a server and redirects the requests to the network server. It is sold as an integral part of the *PC LAN* program and is licensed by Microsoft to other network developers as MS-NET.

- DOS 3.2 is an update of DOS 2 that contains additional function calls to support the NETBIOS.

- NETBIOS is an extension of the ROM BIOS that contains the input and output routines for the network adapter card. With the Token-Ring Network, this is supplied as software loaded into RAM.

- The Adapter Support Interface is software specific to the network adapter card and supports it at the lowest level. These are essentially the "driver" routines for the card.

All five of these programs remain memory-resident when used with any application program. The *PC LAN* program and the Redirector are sold as a unit; the disk operating system must be purchased separately. The Adapter Support Interface is on a disk included with the Adapter Interface Card. The NETBIOS is sold separately.

These programs work together as a unit, as shown in Fig. 4-1. All of the resident network software is loaded and the application program, if used, is loaded on top of this (for a dedicated server, there is no application program).

All the software interfaces in the diagram are well-defined and standardized, making it possible to use other software with the IBM Token-Ring Network hardware or the IBM Token-Ring Network software with other network hardware. In other words, these same components are in just about any DOS network. For example, if you use the 3COM *Network* software, it contains the MS-NET Redirector and fits on top of DOS much as does the *PC LAN* program shown in this illustration. It works with the IBM Token-Ring NETBIOS and the Network Adapter Interface. In the same way, you can use the IBM *PC LAN* software (and the included Redirector) to drive another manufacturer's network hardware—token ring, contention, or whatever. The DOS and DOS NETBIOS interface would all remain the same. The PC Network software really does not care what kind of hardware is being used.

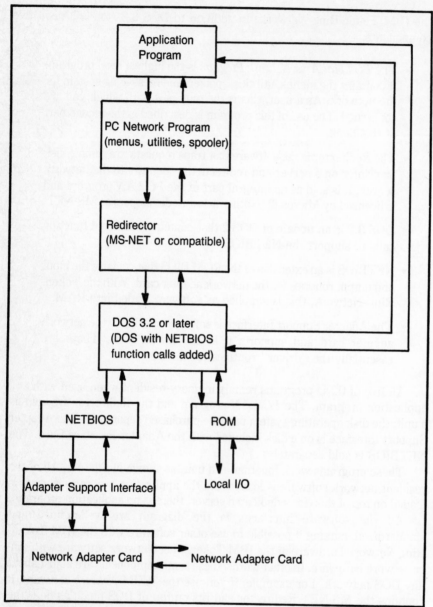

Fig. 4-1. Software layers of a LAN.

When application programs are used with DOS, you will find that some application programs bypass the DOS and access the ROM directly from time to time, speeding up the program. This is often done with the video display, as using DOS to update the video screen with graphics is entirely too slow on an IBM XT when the screen is accessed through the DOS.

In the same way, a programmer writing an application program for a network might speed up the program by accessing the NETBIOS directly and bypassing the DOS. Although a programmer may get by with this for a time, he eventually may get burned if IBM chooses to update the NETBIOS and redefine the DOS/NETBIOS interface. As a user, your concern should be that the application software you purchase will work with all your IBM compatibles now and in the future. You can feel more certain of this if you know the application software works through the DOS.

Chapter 5

LAN Cabling

L OCAL AREA NETWORKS MUST PROVIDE SOME TYPE OF PHYSICAL CHAN-
nel to connect the nodes of the network. The three basic media forms are
coaxial cable, twisted pair, and fiber optics. Each of these has advantages and
disadvantages (see Table 5-1). Whichever you choose, you will also need a
wiring closet.

COAXIAL CABLE

Coaxial cable is one of the most popular methods of connecting nodes in
a LAN. Used widely by cable television systems and other video transmission
systems, coaxial cable is moderate in cost and widely marketed.

The center conductor of a coaxial cable generally is a single wire (although
variations with multiple wires are available). This center conductor is insulated
from an outer shield by plastic, foam, or plastic disks spaced at regular intervals.
The outer shield is either a flexible braid or a semi-rigid metal tube. The entire
cable is covered with a plastic jacket of PVC or Teflon and is 3/8 inch or 1/2
inch thick. This construction provides a reasonably noise-free channel for
network transmission.

Coaxial cables are manufactured to rigid specifications and are available
in many types and sizes. When installing a local area network using this type
of medium, you must be sure that the coaxial cable type matches that specified
by the hardware manufacturer. For example, the 3Com EtherLink network

34

requires an RG-58A/U cable and the IBM PC Network hardware requires an RG-11/U cable. If you already have coaxial cable installed in your building and you wish to use this cable for your LAN, this will limit your selection of network hardware to one that supports the installed cable.

Coaxial cable can be used in both baseband and broadband systems. Broadband media has a bandwidth of 300-400 MHz and can support many channels. Baseband cables support a single channel. Both systems use special connectors to connect the cable to the computer or to other hardware. Coaxial cable cannot be used with the IBM Token-Ring Network.

TWISTED-PAIR CABLE

Twisted-pair is the primary type of media used in telephone systems and has remained the main form of medium for voice communications. To prevent signals on the wire from interfering with adjacent systems and to prevent the adjacent systems from interfering with the network, the pairs of wires are twisted together. The wire is usually made of copper and can be installed with simple tools. Twisted-pair is probably the least expensive of any media alternative.

When developing the IBM Token-Ring Network IBM chose to support a twisted-pair cabling system rather than a coaxial cable system. The wiring system was announced in 1982 and was envisioned as a master cabling plan that businesses could use in their construction building plans, so the buildings could be compatible with IBM's future plans. Most buildings already use extensive twisted-pair cabling systems to support their telephone networks. The traditional twisted-pair wiring is called *voice-grade wiring*, and can be used for IBM's Token-Ring Network—with certain restrictions.

The twisted-pair cable standard, as defined by IBM, includes several types of twisted-pair cable. The types that are relevant to LANs include the following:

- Type 1—Two twisted pairs, each 22 gauge, shielded.

- Type 2—Four pairs of telephone-type twisted-pair wires with a metallic shield and plastic cover.

- Type 3—Telephone-type cable with two or more twisted-pair wires, each 24 gauge.

If you purchase cables from IBM for your network, these will be Type 1 cables. If you use a Type 2 cable, it will work just as well but the extra pairs will not be used. Type 3 is the standard telephone cable already in many buildings. You can use this type with certain restrictions that will be identified in a later section.

Table 5-1. Communications Media and Technology.

Coaxial Cable	Twisted-Pair (Voice Grade)
• Moderate in cost • Large bandwidth (broadband systems can support several channels) • High speed • Good immunity to electrical interference • Well-developed technology	• Low in cost • Poor-to-good immunity to electrical interference • Already exists in many buildings • Baseband use only • Limited speed • Well-developed technology • Easy to install (will fit behind molding in many buildings)

Data-Grade Cable

The Type 1 cable is the method preferred to connect each workstation to a multistation access unit and to connect multistation access units together. The outside of the cable is a black plastic sheath about as big as your little finger. Inside the cable are four solid-copper conductors with plastic insulation, arranged as two twisted pairs, each pair twisted and wrapped in a plastic sheath. You can purchase this cable either in precut lengths, with the connectors installed, or in bulk, from which you can create your own cables.

The Type 1 cable uses a standard DB-9 connector at the end that connects to the workstation. This is a 9-pin connector in the shape of a D—identical to that used to connect a monochrome video monitor to the computer.

The end that connects to the multistation access unit uses a special plastic connector called a *data connector*, especially created by IBM for their wiring system (see Fig. 5-1). The connector is genderless, so there is no need for the usual plug and jack concept. There are no pins on the connector; instead, metal tabs slide past each other and touch. Two plastic locking tabs on each connector engage and prevent the separation of the connectors. To open the connector, lightly squeeze two plates located on the sides of the connector. When you release the plates, the connectors will be locked together. Special locking clips can be used with the connectors to ensure that an accidental squeeze won't separate the connectors. To connect two multistation access units, you would use a cable with the data connectors on each end.

If you wish to build the data-grade wiring into the walls of your building, you can purchase faceplates. The faceplates make it possible to plug a workstation and cable into the faceplates that are installed in the walls. You can then put many faceplates around the work area, each connected by cable to a patch panel at a central wiring closet. Active faceplates are then patched into the multistation access unit in the closet. Workstations are connected to the active faceplates using a cable with a data connector on the end. The maximum distance a workstation can be located from a multistation access unit using data-grade cable is 300 feet.

Twisted Pair (Data Grade)	Fiber Optics
• Moderate in cost • Good immunity to electrical interference • Baseband use only • Moderate speed • Limited suppliers and availability	• High in cost • Excellent noise immunity • Very high speed and bandwidth • Still maturing technology

Standard Type 1 cable is not designed for outdoor use, but a Type 1 outdoor cable is available. The cable is not self-supporting, and if outdoor cable is used it should be lashed to a supporting *messenger wire*. Special grounding precautions must be observed (see the *IBM Cabling System Planning and*

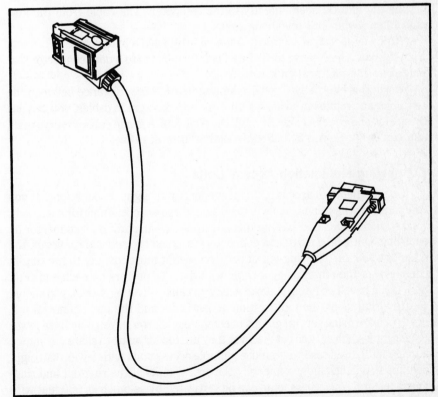

Fig. 5-1. Cable to connect a workstation to a MAU. Courtesy of International Business Machines Corporation.

Installation Guide). If Type 1 outdoor cable is used indoors, it must be installed in conduit.

IBM cables function between −40 degrees and 176 degrees Fahrenheit. They should not be immersed in water. Cables should not be closer than 5 inches to unshielded power lines supporting 2000 watts or less (24 inches at 5000 watts), but can be in the same conduit with telephone wires if the other wires carry only telephone signals. Avoid running network cable parallel to electrical cable for any distance. Typical maximum limits are 30 feet with a 2-inch separation and 15 feet for a 1-inch separation.

Voice-Grade Cable

You can also use voice-grade cable (Type 3) for the network if you take certain precautions. Because the voice-grade lines are not shielded you must use a special low-pass filter between the computer and the cable. This filters out the high-frequency part of the digital signal that would radiate from the cable and interfere with other devices. The low-pass filter has a DB-9 connector on one end and connects directly to the computer. The cable from the low-pass filter is standard telephone cable.

At the multistation access unit end you will need a patch cable to connect from the patch box where the twisted pair terminates to a data connector that plugs into the multistation access unit.

Using this alternative, you are limited to a 150-foot distance between the computer and multistation access unit. As with data-grade cables, you can use faceplates and run the cable through the wall. Voice-grade cable is very small, and can easily be run behind the molding in most offices.

Connecting Multistation Access Units

One multistation access unit can support up to eight workstations. If you need more workstations, you will need an additional access unit for each eight workstations. Each unit has eight connectors plus an additional connector on each end. One of the extra end connectors is called the *ring-out connector*, the other is a *ring-in*. The ring-out of one access unit must connect to the ring-in connector of the other, using a cable with data connectors on each end (Fig. 5-2). If you have two units, you will need two cables. In other words, you should create a ring using the multistation access units and the end connectors.

If you are using several groups of computers (clusters), you may have fewer than eight in each cluster but discover they are too far apart to share a common access unit. In this case you can use multiple access units with fewer than eight computers on each unit, connecting the access units at the ring-out and ring-in connectors. The access units can be separated by as much as 650 feet with data-grade cable and 400 feet with voice-grade cable.

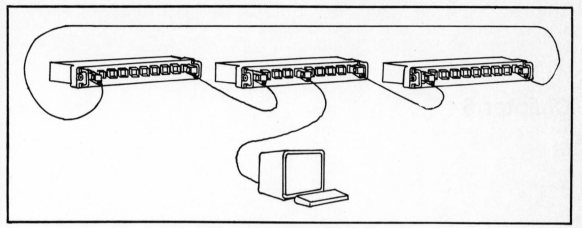

Fig. 5-2. Connecting MAUs together. Courtesy of International Business Machines Corporation.

FIBER OPTICS

Fiber optic conductors are small pipes made by depositing layers of pure silicon on the inner surface of a glass tube about three feet long. When the layers are complete, the tube is drawn into a thin strand of transparent glass. The optics are controlled so precisely that the resulting strand can conduct a light signal from one end to the other over a distance of a mile with almost no loss in intensity.

Fiber optic cables can transmit very high bandwidths over long distances with almost complete immunity to interference. The only disadvantage is the cost, which at the present time is quite high. If distance is a problem, however, a fiber optic repeater is available for the IBM Token-Ring Network that extends the radius of a network much further than can be achieved with conventional cable.

THE WIRING CLOSET

A wiring closet is a concentration point for the cables of the network. The wiring closet contains any multistation access units, patch panels, and other equipment useful at a concentration point. In a small network, there is only a single multistation access unit and perhaps no real wiring closet. The MAU can be attached to a wall, pushed behind a bookcase, or located near a server or workstation central to the network. In larger systems there may be multiple MAUs, patch panels, and other equipment located in one or more wiring closets. The temperature of the wiring closet (or MAU environment) must be between 50 degrees and 150 degrees Fahrenheit.

Chapter 6

Rules and Conventions

A LOCAL AREA NETWORK IS A METHOD FOR PASSING COMMUNICATIONS between computers. Whenever a communication occurs, rules and conventions control the process. Imagine a committee meeting in which each member wishes to speak. To prevent mass confusion rules are adopted. If someone wishes to speak he may raise his hand. The chairperson recognizes the person who wishes to speak, and then that person has the floor. No one can speak who has not been recognized by the chairperson. The rules and conventions for the committee meeting are called *protocols*.

In the same way protocols exist that are the rules or standards for computer communications. These standards, or protocols, are defined in a hierarchy of layers. The detailed nature of these layers will not be pursued in this book, but it will be helpful to gain at least some understanding of their function so you may manage your network more efficiently.

The concept of a hierarchy of layers as applied to communication standards is not limited to data communications alone. In communicating to the reader of this book I use technical terms. There must be a common understanding or definition of each of these technical terms or communication will not take place. This application-specific vocabulary is the highest level of protocol in our communication, and we might call this the "application level."

The next level might refer to the semantics and language I use. This might be called the "presentation layer." Someone with a good knowledge of English could proofread the book at this level without knowing very much about the subject of the book or the meaning of the technical terms.

At the next level we might refer to standards that apply to packaging the information. For example, my publisher requires this book to be in a certain form (or standard) for submission. Main headings have to be identified in a specific way, subheadings similarly identified, and the location for figures, listings, and tables defined.

We could continue this look at layering, applying standards and function definitions at each layer. The same is true for data communications. Through the years and work of many people, seven data communication layers and the protocols for each layer have been defined. These seven layers can be applied to data communications between the computer and a peripheral (such as a printer), to long-haul communications (using a modem), and to the transfer of data between programs, such as between two word processors.

These seven layers exist for all LANs, regardless of type or manufacture. The fact that standards exist for each level ensures compatibility between vendors and the various software and hardware that exists to support local area networking.

Local area network functions and control are implemented in seven layers. The seven layers, with their hierarchy, are shown in Fig. 6-1. At the highest level is the Application Level, the level of most concern to users. The discussion of this level (which includes the *PC Local Area Network* program) makes up the larger part of this book. At the lowest level is the Physical Layer, which also occupies a major portion of this book. In between are five other layers that are important for the functioning of the network, but their support is less visible to the user and they are only briefly mentioned in this book.

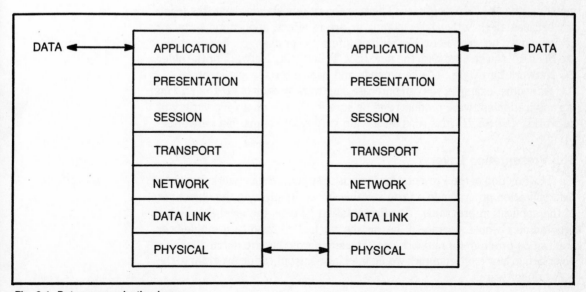

Fig. 6-1. Data communication layers.

Layers function independently of each other, and each layer has a defined function. The implementation of any layer can be changed without substantially affecting the other layers. The network software, for example, can be changed without affecting either the application software (Application layer) or the hardware (the Physical layer) if the network is properly designed.

Standards also mean it is relatively easy to upgrade a network as new technology is available. The hardware can be changed (in the ideal case) without affecting other aspects of the network (such as the application software or the network software).

THE SEVEN LAYERS

Data are packaged by each layer in a certain form. Once packaged, the data are sent to the next layer above or below it for processing. At each layer we may add or subtract certain control data to the basic data for performing the function of that layer. You might think of the basic data being transferred as the raw data, and many of the layers add additional bytes to the data according to the standard for that layer. The end result is a "package" of data that is passed to the next layer for processing. Let's look at the function and role of each of these layers in more detail.

The Application Layer

The Application layer is the one at which the user generally operates. These standards refer to the application software that functions on the network, including the *PC LAN* software. There are very few standards at this level, but because all the other layer standards are in effect, application software can be moved between networks with no alteration or changes. For example, the *PC LAN* can be used with the new IBM Token-Ring Network or the older PC Network hardware. The commands and user interface are identical.

As another example, you can purchase a network version of *dBASE III Plus* (an application software product) and be sure it will run on a wide variety of networks. *dBASE III Plus* runs on a wide variety of compatible networks.

The Presentation Layer

The function of the Presentation layer is to support the network functions for application programs in a form suitable for accomplishing the objectives of the application programs. The Presentation layer is the level at which a programmer would operate if he or she wished to modify a single-user application program for network use. The standards that are defined for this layer define how a programmer would interface an application program to the network software.

The major DOS functions a programmer uses in this layer were provided in DOS release 3.1, which was written for IBM by Microsoft. For the IBM Token-Ring Network, DOS 3.1 was modified slightly and released as DOS 3.2. The network functions are defined in IBM's *PC Network Technical Manual.*

For network operation there is an additional level of functions that must be added to the DOS. These functions support the redirecting of disk and print requests from the workstation to the server when necessary. For example, suppose the user wishes to load a file stored on the hard disk of the server. This might be disk C of the server. Assume the user has a hard disk C and has assigned the server hard disk as disk D on the local workstation. Each time the user requests a file from D on the local workstation, the request must be redirected to C on the server hard disk.

The software to support these redirecting functions was written by Microsoft and sold as *MS-NET.* This *redirector shell* is loaded into memory as a resident program and actually sits on top of DOS when the network is active. You do not purchase *MS-NET.* Vendors selling LAN software purchase the rights to *MS-NET* from Microsoft and include this as an integral part of the product. *MS-NET* is already included in the IBM *PC LAN* software. *MS-NET* is also included as a part of other network software, such as 3COM's *3Plus.*

At other times, vendors will choose to write their own redirector (and perhaps even DOS), trying to emulate the Microsoft products. An example of this is Novell's *Netware.*

As a user, your main concern at this level is that you have a standard network redirection interface that will work with your application software. For example, if you are using *dBASE III Plus*, you would want to be sure your version of *dBASE III Plus* works with the DOS and the redirector your network will be using. If you plan to purchase a network version of a word processor in a year or two, can you be sure this will work with the network software you purchase now? If a future DOS is released that supports more memory, will your network be obsolete? Using a product that merely emulates the *MS-NET* function may buy you speed now, but could cause incompatibility problems with some of your current software or future releases of current software.

Using the Microsoft products (DOS 3.2 and a LAN that includes the *MS-NET* redirector) means you can be certain of future compatibility, but may result in slower throughput and fewer features when the network is compared with other networks. When planning your network, these are some of the trade-offs you will need to consider when making the decision and purchasing your hardware and software.

In other types of data communication environments, the Presentation layer controls the highest level of overhead and data formatting external to the raw data itself. For example, in transmitting data to a printer the presentation layer defines machine control functions, such as the tabbing and form feed codes. In transferring a file between two word processors, the Presentation layer defines the format of the word processing file.

The Session Layer

The Session layer provides the functions for supporting a particular session. This would include the user identification, passwords, and priority control. At this level the data are packaged as a *packet*, and the packet is assembled in the computer memory using commands for transmission on the network.

Programmers can work at this level to interface a program to the network, but it is the lowest level accessible by a programmer writing application programs. The functions needed for this level are provided in the NETBIOS program provided with the IBM Token-Ring Adapter card. In other networks (such as the PC Network hardware), the NETBIOS is provided as firmware, i.e., as a chip on the adapter card. It functions much as an extension to the ROM on the computer motherboard.

You should use caution when purchasing any application software that interfaces directly at the NETBIOS level. Although this level has been defined as a standard by IBM, and software designed to support this standard should be compatible in other networks, there is no guarantee of compatibility in the future. It is much like writing an application program and bypassing the DOS calls, using ROM directly. A programmer may get by with it for awhile, but sooner or later hardware changes may cause software incompatibility. Just as IBM has changed their ROM periodically, we can expect the NETBIOS to change and evolve in future versions of network software.

The Transport Layer

Any given message may consist of several packets. In the Transport layer protocol, bytes are added to the transmission of packets within a single session to identify the packet. This permits multiple packets and sessions to be on the line, and yet the destination computer can reassemble the packets of a particular session in the correct order.

The Network Layer

The Network layer controls the flow of the packet through the network or between networks. Bytes defining the source node and the destination node are added, as well as identifiers defining the source and destination network. This makes it possible for a packet to be transmitted correctly even from one network to another through any gateways that may exist.

The Data Link Layer

At the Data Link level the data is defined in *frames*. Several bytes are added at the end of the frame to permit error checking in the transmission. The standards at this level provide for retransmission if a frame is not received correctly. Bytes indicating the source address and destination address are added (these are different from the node identifiers added at the Network layer.) It is the destination address added at this level that is checked by the receiving station to see if the frame is intended for that station or not. Once the destination station determines that the frame is intended for it, it uses the source address to determine where to send the acknowledgement.

The Physical Layer

The function of the Physical layer is to provide the means of transmitting the data from the source node to the destination node. Standards at this level define the cable, the connectors, and topology constraints.

LAYER FUNCTIONS IN THE IBM TOKEN-RING NETWORK

In the IBM Token-Ring Network the adapter card handles processing only for the Data Link layer, leaving the processing for the Session, Transport, and Network layers to the processor in the computer. This is in sharp contrast to the adapter for the older IBM PC Network hardware, which handles processing for all four layers. The result is that the IBM Token-Ring Network is only slightly faster than the PC Network hardware. The throughput speed of the IBM Token-Ring Network is estimated at 750K bits/second, against the PC Network hardware's 680K bits/second.

Note: Since each level functions independently of the others, it is entirely possible that vendors could move processing of other layers to the adapter card as the technology improves.

Chapter 7

Planning for the LAN

PLANNING FOR A LOCAL AREA NETWORK BEGINS LONG BEFORE THE EQUIP-
ment is purchased. Basic needs must be assessed, goals must be defined,
and resources inventoried. This chapter will give you some insights into this
planning.

WHAT ARE THE GOALS?

The first step should be defining the goals to be achieved by the network.
You should identify the functional purpose of the network and be sure a LAN
is the best method for achieving these objectives. You should also ascertain
whether the IBM Token-Ring Network is the best LAN for your purposes.

Network information processing generally falls into two broad categories:
transaction-based processing and sequential processing. *Sequential processing*
refers to the serial transfer of data to or from disk files. The data transfer is
normally infrequent and occurs in lengthy bursts. The demands on the network
are minimal, because most of the processing is at the local workstation. Typical
sequential applications include word processing, spreadsheets, printing files,
and copying files.

Transaction-based processing refers to network management of data that
is transferred with files that are randomly accessed. In this case, data transfer
to or from files is almost continuous, and the demands on the network are at
a maximum. The most common applications of transaction-based processing
are database management and program development.

One of your early goals should be to define whether your network processing will be primarily sequential or transaction-based. Transaction-based processing generally puts much more of a demand on the network management and involves more care in network planning and in the application software selection.

Here are some questions that are important in goal definition:

1. What functions need to be networked (accounting, database, word processing, spreadsheet, etc.)? What are the priorities?

2. Are you primarily concerned with sending and receiving messages, sharing programs, sharing data, or sharing hardware resources?

3. What are the primary factors driving your decision to implement a LAN? (Why can you not, for example, simply move floppy disks between computers or add extra printers?)

Before the network decision is made you should take the time to study various alternatives in meeting your needs, including the possibility of upgrading to a larger multiuser system (see Chapter 1). Examine several different types of LANs.

If you decide to pursue the LAN alternative, compare several networks and make your decision objectively, based on your goals. Here are some of the advantages of the IBM Token-Ring alternative:

- Based on a viable standard.

- Fully supports IBM hardware and DOS standard.

- Includes the *MS-NET* redirector, giving the user a standard software interface for application programs.

- Open architecture invites third-party participation at all levels (adapters, gateways, cabling, etc.).

- Implementation based on CCITT ISO-OSI standards.

- Lower in cost than most competitors.

- Ease of installation.

- Inexpensive cable alternatives and baseband support.

- Ease of use.

- Good fault tolerance.

The IBM approach also has some disadvantages:

- Less throughput speed than some competitive networks.

- Gateway support to larger systems announced, but not yet available.

- Limited availability of access security control.

- Limited file and record locking.

- No built-in data encryption.

- No disk cache. Information transferred to or from the disk is transferred directly, without keeping recently used "pages" in memory. This reduces throughput, making the system slower than competitive systems (such as Novell's) that use a disk cache.

- Baseband operation may impose limitations if broadband support is needed (if broadband cable system is already installed or dictated by what the channel must support).

- Primarily supports IBM hardware.

DEFINING THE LIMITS

In planning your system, you must plan for both short-term and long-term objectives:

- What is the number of users the network will support?

- What is the number of printers the network will support?

- How many servers will be used? Will they also serve as workstations? How many hard disks will be in the system? What is the capacity of each?

EXAMINE YOUR PRIORITIES

Since the IBM Token-Ring Network is a peer-to-peer system with no host, you can install it incrementally. For example, you can start with a few workstations and a single server that is also a workstation. Later you can add more workstations and eliminate using the server as a workstation. Still later, you may wish to add a second server. Examine your priorities when starting and plan your system growth relative to these. For example, your primary priority may be one of the following:

- Sharing data for one or more programs.

- Sharing programs.

- Sharing hardware resources such as printers.

- Improving internal communications.

- Remote communications.

Focus on meeting your primary objective first, then add other objectives as you become more familiar with the network.

SURVEYING THE NEED

Take a user survey of what user needs are and what they expect of the network. A sample survey form is shown in Fig. 7-1. Once this is completed, use it to document a network specification that can be submitted to a vendor. A sample form to fill out for a vendor is shown in Fig. 7-2.

Problems that may seem trivial may become the key to important decisions. Consider the example of a corporation installing a network and trying to decide what paper to use in a laser printer shared on the network. The users all had special needs: letterhead, forms, and plain paper in both standard and legal

---

USER SURVEY FOR LOCAL AREA NETWORK INSTALLATION

1. Could you use access to a local area network?

2. How could you use the network?
   a) Send and receive electronic mail
   b) To share data files with another user (transfer between systems)
   c) To share an application program with other users
   d) To have more storage capacity
   e) To share a printer
   f) To access a minicomputer (or mainframe)
   g) To use a common data file with another user
   h) To access computer from off-site
   (Prioritize if you have several answers, marking the most important with "1," the next with "2," etc.)

3. What application software do you use the most? What other application software do you also use?

4. What hardware do you use? (IBM XT, AT, printers?)

5. Do you have a specific hardware or software need?

Fig. 7-1. The user questionnaire. Courtesy of International Business Machines Corporation.

LOCAL AREA NETWORK SUMMARY REPORT FOR VENDOR

Company Name: _____

Address: _____

City: _____ State _____ Zip _____

1. What is your network preference?

2. What systems will you be using for a server? How many servers will you need? Will each be a print or file server?

3. How many printers will be on the network? How will they be distributed on the servers?

4. How many workstations will you be using immediately? Within a year?

5. What is each workstation description? (Describe hardware, memory, and disk storage.)

6. Is any cabling system already installed? If so, what type is it?

7. Does any off-site equipment need to be interfaced to the network? If so, what is the equipment?

8. Does the network need to interface with any host computer? If so, what type?

9. What is the major goal of the network?

10. What other goals must be supported?

11. What application software must be supported?

12. What is the level of workstation user experience that can be expected (novice, intermediate, advanced)?

13. What level of vendor support is needed?
    a) Cabling
    b) Installation
    c) Training
    d) Consulting
    e) Maintenance

Fig. 7-2. Vendor summary.

sizes. The company might use the messaging system to tell the operator what to load, but what if the print queue is long? In this case the operator might not be able to change the paper quickly enough, or might put in the wrong paper. The alternatives would be to use a second printer, keep the queue short, or keep the paper choices minimal.

NETWORK LOADING

One concern for anyone planning a network is its efficiency. If there are too many users using too few servers with a lot of data transferred over the network, the network is going to bog down and everyone will be disappointed. This will be true on any type of network, whether it is an IBM Token-Ring Network or a big mainframe host system with users supported by a star topology from the mainframe. I have seen large systems with expensive mainframe equipment frustrate users because of long delays. The delay is variable and unpredictable, which frustrates a user even more. This means you should do some figuring ahead of time to determine whether your network will actually help or hinder the users, and plan the network carefully so these delays are not experienced.

As an aid to planning, IBM has defined a "standard load," shown in Table 7-1. This is a hypothetical mix of various activities from a workstation that is defined as one load. The criterion of satisfactory performance was defined as a 90 percent probability that if a user made a network request from a workstation it would be serviced *at once*. Since the IBM AT and IBM XT have different transfer rates, IBM defined *at once* slightly differently for the two machines. For the PC XT, the criterion was no network activity in progress

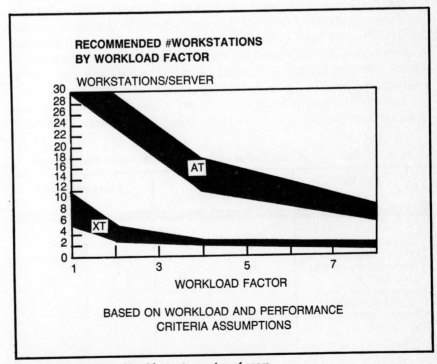

Fig. 7-3. Relationship of load factor to number of users.

when the request is received. For the IBM AT the criterion was no network activity queued, or waiting to be executed. Figure 7-3 shows the relationship between the load factor and the number of users for both the IBM PC XT and the IBM AT. For each machine, a band (or upper and lower limit) is shown, as it is very difficult to judge this with complete accuracy. Table 7-2 shows the number of workstations supported by IBM's Token-Ring Network.

From the relationship we can draw a few assumptions for a network with moderate loading:

1. An IBM XT server can support 6 to 12 users if the load is moderate, and 4 users under with a load factor of three.

2. The IBM AT server can support 30 users with a load factor of one, and 18 to 22 users if the load factor is increased to three.

Notice that the load factor for this test was defined as entirely *sequential* processing. If your plans include mostly transaction-based processing, you will probably place heavier demands on the network. If your applications include database management and you need to use the slower IBM XT for a server, you may wish to modify your programs so that transfers are more sequentially oriented. For example, you could create a batch file at a workstation, transfer it to a server, and then let the server process the batch file (perhaps even when the network is less busy). Computers are cheap compared to time lost if users are kept waiting. For this reason you may find it cost-effective to increase the number of servers, discourage the use of a server as a workstation, or to convert a server from an IBM XT to an IBM AT.

Table 7-2 is a general summary guide that shows the suggested number of workstations that can be used in an IBM Token-Ring Network. This should

Table 7-1. Definition of Load Factor as Applied to IBM Token-Ring Network.

Activity	Kilobytes of Data Transferred	Times per Hour
Load a program	64	6
Load spreadsheet data	2	3
Save spreadsheet data	2	2
Load text file	12	3
Save text file	12	2
Send a message	0.5	4
Receive a message	0.5	4
Print a file	4	2

Table 7-2. Number of Network Workstations Supported by IBM Token-Ring Network.

Access Type	IBM XT	IBM AT	Special*
Random access (data base management, program development)	2-3	4-8	10-15
Mixed access (accounting)	4-6	10-15	18-30
Serial access (word processing, spreadsheets)	5-10	6-25	20-80
* Support using special servers, such as 3Com's 3Server.			

only be used as a planning aid, as other variables can influence the limits. For example:

- What is the clock speed in the server? If the server is an IBM XT with an enhancement board, it may support a few more users than one without, but do not expect much improvement. The disk access speed is still the same. Enhancement boards with a disk cache will show improvement. An 8 MHz IBM AT will perform better than a 6 MHz AT.

- What is the true load factor? A network supporting primarily serial transfers can still be heavily loaded if users are working with a lot of small files or doing a lot of file reading or writing.

GETTING THE DETAILS

When making plans for your LAN, you will need to create a detailed list of everything you need for your network. The next few paragraphs describe a typical shopping list for the IBM Token-Ring Network.

For each workstation you will need:

- One IBM Token-Ring Network PC Adapter (Part #6339100)

- One DB9-to-token-ring data-grade connector cable (Part #6339088) or, if you plan to use telephone wiring, a DB9-to-modular connector with a low-pass filter.

- DOS 3.20 or later

- *IBM PC Network Program* version 1.10 or later (Part #6024195)

- *IBM Token-Ring NETBIOS Program* (Part #6467037)

For each eight workstations or servers you will need:

- IBM 8228 Multistation Access Unit

- Patch cable with data-grade connectors at each end (Part #8642551)

You should also purchase two DB9-to-data connector cables for prototyping the network with two systems independent of the installed wiring for test purposes. You may also wish to purchase some of these additional components:

- Data connectors (Part #8310574)

- Data connector faceplates (part #8310572 or 4760486)

- Wiring concentrator (Part #6091077)

- Distribution panel (Part #8642520)

- Jumper cable (Part #8310554)

Note: For a complete network installation in a corporate environment, the shopping list can be extensive and you may need the help of a professional network installer. For more details of what is involved in the cable installation, consult the following IBM publications:

GA27-3677-1, *Token-Ring Network: Introduction and Planning Guide*

GA27-3678-0, *Token-Ring Network: Installation Guide.*

Hardware Resources

Check your current resources and determine what you can use in the network and what you will need to purchase. The IBM Token-Ring Network works on "IBM-compatible" computers. Unfortunately, if you are using a clone or some of the so-called PC-compatibles, you might find the IBM Token-Ring Network does not work on your system, or that you need to make changes in the system (such as purchasing a new ROM). Do your research early to discover what problems exist with the system you are using.

If you are using a compatible, will DOS 3.2 boot up on your system? Can you identify other users who are using your type of hardware with the IBM Token-Ring Network? What problems have they had? Are you using a specially formatted hard disk (these may not work with the network)? How old is the

ROM chip in each network computer (you may have to upgrade some ROMs)? How much memory is in any system that you plan to use for a server?

Note: Compaq Portable ROMs should be Version F or later. IBM PC ROMs are more tolerant: a 1982 ROM will probably work.

You should plan to expand each server to 640K. You may also wish to add hard disks to workstations that are currently floppy-disk only or expand a workstation memory size.

Define the configuration you will use for each system. Under the IBM *PC LAN Program* a computer can have any one of four configurations: server, messenger, receiver, and redirector. In a small network you would probably install one system as a server and the remaining systems as messengers.

The server must have a hard disk. Part of the disk will be allocated to a public directory. There will also be a private directory for each user on the disk. The public directory contains programs that are available to everyone on the network. When a user at a workstation wishes to execute a program on a public directory, it is loaded directly from the server disk to the workstation memory through the network. The file attributes of these programs on the server disk are set to read-only so that the programs cannot be erased by a user. It is not necessary for the user to have a copy of the program on a local disk.

The private subdirectory for each user contains data files and other data that is not available to other users. Although each user's private area is generally relatively small, if there are many users the total private space can be as much as the public area.

The IBM AT is a much faster server than an IBM XT. It is generally best to work toward keeping the server as a server and not using it as a workstation. Using a server as a workstation will slow down network activity. You should also remember that if it is used as a workstation and it crashes, it will bring the entire network down.

You can connect several printers to a single server, but the IBM Token-Ring Network can only support printing on a single printer at a time. If several print jobs are waiting to be printed on a server with several printers, each will print, one at a time, on the appropriate printer. If you need to keep two or more printers busy at the same time, each printer must be put on a separate server.

Memory Requirements

The following are the general memory requirements for each configuration. These figures include a 64K memory allocation for application programs or external commands.

Server	309K
Messenger	245K

Receiver	181K
Redirector	117K

This figure includes the 46K needed for the NETBIOS and 7K for the adapter interface software. Actual memory requirements will vary depending upon the values of the startup parameters.

Software Resources

Examine your current software for network support. Some single-user software may work on a network, but will be limited to a single user at a time. Some single-user software has been specifically modified so it will not work on a network at all, even with a single user. Check for network support with each of your software suppliers. This should also include software you plan to purchase (see Appendix C).

If your organization plans to endorse application software to use on the network you will want to plan for products that offer network support. Some products offer better network support than others. For example, several database managers support networks, but some do it better than others.

Programs that are copy-protected or require a key disk should only be used on a network if absolutely necessary. Many copy-protected programs must be uninstalled before a hard disk can be backed up. A disk crash or a careless backup can mean the program is completely unretrievable. You are safer by avoiding such programs or using a special copy utility program that can create copies of your protected programs that require no key disk or special uninstallation to use.

Examine your programs to see how much memory space each is using. Be sure your network software will fit in memory with the application software you are using and the workstation configuration you plan to use.

Resident programs may or may not work on a network. If you are heavily dependent upon one or more resident programs, check their operation with the network before committing yourself.

Cable Planning

You should check to see what wiring currently exists in your building. If cable exists, will it work for the network? If you plan to add cables, measure the amount you will need. Draw up cabling diagrams. Be sure that the distances you propose are within the limits established by IBM (Table 7-3). Plan where you will locate your multiaccess station units.

Remember that in most companies people move every couple of years or so. Plan for growth and change, based on past experience in your company. It is not unusual, when installing cable, to install twice as many cable connections as necessary to prepare for expansion.

Table. 7-3. Maximum Distances for Cables in an IBM Token-Ring Network.

	Data Grade	Voice Grade
PC to MAU (Maximum)	1000'	330'
(Recommended maximum)	330'	150'
Maximum number of MAU Clusters	12	2
MAU Cluster-to-Cluster (Maximum)	650'	400'

To plan your cables, draw up a floor plan showing all relevant detail. This should be done regardless of the size of the network. For even a two-computer system there should be a cable plan. It will help you define the length of cables needed, or even decide whether the system will work. This information can also be used to determine the cost of the cables, which should be a part of the initial proposal and budget. Draw the plan to scale.

Define a numbering system and number all MAUs, cables, and each equipment piece for planning reference. The numbering system should be designed so that the cable number tells you information about the source MAU and destination workstation. You may want cables located between wiring closets to have a certain numbering designation, and have cables leading to workstations to use a different designation.

In your planning, remember that the maximum cable run from a MAU to a workstation for a Type 1 cable is 330 feet (100 meters). Intercloset wiring (between MAUs) is limited to a 660-foot length.

THE HUMAN FACTOR

It is a good idea to define some testing method for objectively measuring the network operation against your goals. For example, you may be using a particular database manager and plan to share data among workstations once the network is installed. The application is heavily transaction-based, with four users entering and editing data constantly during the day. You are currently using four IBM XT machines and plan to make one a server and use the other three with the server as workstations. From what we have already said, you can see that this network is going to be a little slow. You may wish to invest in an IBM-AT for a server and use all four IBM XTs as workstations.

Before committing your money and time, you may wish to set up your software on a demonstration system (or another system in which the network is already operational) to measure the effectiveness of the system. If this is not possible, you may wish to work with the vendor to make the sale of the hardware and software contingent upon your acceptance of some objective, defined criterion.

Defining Human Resources

You should also define the skills and talents you have available. These can be roughly defined in four categories: the administrator, the system integrator, the server operator, and the users. In some systems, one person may have two or three roles. The roles should be defined during the planning process, and the administrator and system integrator should be involved at the planning level.

The Administrator. The administrator has the responsibility for general network support. The administrator defines conventions and determines who will use which resources. The administrator also defines what resources will be shared on the network and which must be supported locally. The administrator is a single authority with the responsibility for network decisions: what software will be used, when backups will be done, which systems are servers, and where programs and data are stored. The administrator does not need to have network access unless he or she is also a user or server operator.

The System Integrator. The system integrator has the technical responsibility for the network. He or she may be from within the organization, a paid consultant, or perhaps even the person who is selling you the network. The system integrator has the responsibility for the technical aspects of the planning and installation.

The Server Operator. The server operator has the responsibility for the operation of one or more server machines. The responsibilities include responding to user messages, checking the network status, backing up the disk, tuning the systems, and physically checking printers (ribbons, paper, etc.).

Programming and developmental work should never be done on a server machine. If the server goes down, it will take all the users down with it. If the server operator needs to do developmental work, it should be done at a workstation.

The amount of time required for the server operator to support the server depends upon several factors, including whether the server is a workstation, the number of printers, and the workload at the server. In most applications you will find it takes several hours a day, and in some cases is a full-time job.

The User. The user has the responsibility for one or more workstations. This includes the support of any local printers, backup of any local hard disk, and responding to messages from the server operator. The user needs to have an awareness of both the operating system and the network software.

It is really not necessary for the users to have special technical training in order for them to make use of the network. If a user has had DOS experience already, generally another half day of orientation is enough to get a user familiar with the basics of network operation. With *PC LAN* it is possible for users to use menus to execute most of the commands. The user need only call up the menu and select the desired function.

Allocating Users and Servers

One important aspect of keeping the network throughput good is the allocation of users and servers. If you have a dozen users and they are all using a single server, this is not as efficient as distributing the workload over several servers. Whether you have several servers and a dozen users or only three users and a single server, you will still need to do some planning to determine what will be done on the local workstations and what will be done on the server. The proper planning of what data and programs are on each system is an important aspect of making sure the network runs efficiently. You should start with an initial plan, but once the network is in operation you will probably wish to try various alternatives to see if they help productivity.

The server directory configuration is normally defined using the installation aid that comes with the *PC Local Area Network Program.* Before using the aid, however, you should define the directories you wish to install.

Each server needs a public directory that is accessible to everyone on the network. This is generally called the APPS directory in the IBM Token-Ring Network. It contains shared programs with their attributes set to read-only so no one can erase them. There may also be some common data files in this directory.

Each server also contains one or more private directories. These can only be used by specific users. Generally you will have one private directory for each user. If you have several servers, the private directories can be distributed over the servers with the work load approximately equal on each server. You are also limited by the fact that a server can support a maximum of 25 users at one time. (There may be more users than this on a network with one server, but only 25 can use the server at one time. If you have a large number of users, plan for multiple servers.) This is a limit imposed by the system tables in the *PC LAN* program.

You may wish to create departmental directories on some of the servers. These are directories with departmental data files and special programs accessible to a group of users.

As a final step, plan printer, gateway, and modem resources that will be a part of the system.

Using a word processor or spreadsheet, document your directory plans. Keep this documentation and update it as you make changes or add workstations.

SELECTING YOUR VENDOR

Purchasing a network is considerably different from purchasing a computer or printer. A network purchase requires much, much more support. The learning curve is steep.

If you connect the network and find it does not work, what or who gets the blame? You have cables, DOS, hardware, application software, computers and adapter cards. Tracking down an elusive problem from nothing more than a cryptic error message can discourage even an experienced person.

For this reason you should choose your vendor carefully. The better stores will have salespeople trained about the particular type of network you are purchasing. You may also wish to purchase some consulting time from them at the early planning stages, through the installation. Some vendors may require the purchase of some of their consulting time with the sale of the network.

Chapter 8

Using the Disk Operating System

IN USING A NETWORK, THE DOS ENVIRONMENT IS CHANGED. CERTAIN COMmands are no longer available, such as the CHKDSK command. New commands are available as a part of the *PC Local Area Network Program.*

Before installing the network, let us look at the DOS operating system and its relationship to the network.

USING BATCH FILES

Computers (both the personal and the large mainframe varieties) operate in one of two modes: batch or interactive. In the interactive mode, the system takes a command entered by the user and immediately executes the command. Most microcomputer users primarily work in the interactive mode. The IBM PC/XT/AT computers indicate they are in the interactive mode and waiting for a command by displaying a prompt, such as:

C >

Sometimes, however, we wish to automate processes and store a collection of commands that will accomplish a desired objective as a file. A DOS file that contains one or more DOS commands is called a *batch* file. Batch files are used for initializing the computer on starting, backing up a collection of files, compiling programs, and other tasks that lend themselves to automated procedures.

61

Batch files always are named with a BAT file extension, such as WS.BAT. The user enters only the first part of the file name, and the computer automatically locates and executes the batch file if it exists.

It is generally advantageous to use a batch file to start most application programs. In a single-user system, the batch file is kept on a BAT directory. Once it is initiated, it switches the system to the appropriate subdirectory, loads any special program (keyboard enhancers, mouse drivers, etc.), then loads the application program. In a real sense, the batch file customizes the application program for the user. For example, to start *Symphony* you might have the batch file ACC.BAT in the root (or main) directory that contains the following:

```
CD \ SYMPH
MENU 123
PROKEY \ Q
ACCESS
PROKEY \ I
CD \
```

This switches the computer to the *Symphony* subdirectory, loads the mouse driver, turns off the Prokey enhancer, and then starts *Symphony*.

On a network server, a single program may be shared by many users. A BATCH subdirectory contains all the batch files for the server operator, and each private subdirectory contains a BATCH subdirectory with the batch files for starting the application programs for that user. The PATH command must be modified to permit access to these batch files (see next section).

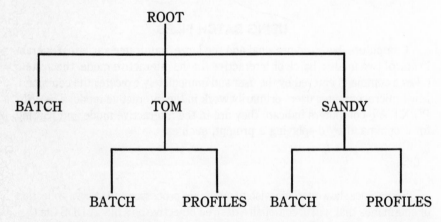

Batch file names can have any name that is convenient, but are limited by the eight-letter constraints of DOS. Using short names makes it easy to start your favorite programs. Batch files can be created with any editor and can be displayed with the Type command.

The PATH Command

If you enter a program name and no PATH command has been specified, DOS examines only the current directory for the command. For example, if your *dBASE III* program is in DB, you are in the DB subdirectory; enter:

```
C > DBASE    < Enter >
```

DOS searches only the current DB directory for the DBASE program. Since the program is in the current subdirectory, the program will load and execute. If you are in another directory, you will get the message: "Invalid command or file name."

With a network system, files are in many directories. The PATH command permits you to search several directories for any specified file. The PATH command can be put in AUTOEXEC.BAT, executed each time the system is booted. For example, suppose the following command is added to the starting batch file:

```
PATH = C: \ ;C: \ BATCH;C: \ APPS \ NETWORK;C: \ APPS \ DOS
```

After this command has been issued, DOS will search each of the directories specified, in the order specified, in an attempt to find the program. DOS will begin its search in the current directory. This is always true, regardless of the path specified. If the file cannot be found in the current directory, the search is continued in the C: root directory, then in BATCH, then in \ APPS \ NETWORK, and finally in APPS \ DOS. Only if it fails to find the program in all five named directories will the error message be displayed.

Use caution in specifying the PATH chain. If you specify a long path name and later make a typographical error entering the program name, it will take DOS considerable time to search all directories for the non-existent file.

Note: The PATH command only works with COM, EXE, and BAT files. If you are using a program that contains overlay or data files, PATH will not help you find the rest of the program. For example, if you use a path file to load *WordStar* (WS.COM) from a subdirectory you are not using, you will find that *WordStar* quickly stops. The *WordStar* overlay files will not load. The PATH command also cannot be used to locate data files. If you wish to edit a file called TEST.DOC, you must be in the same directory as TEST.DOC regardless of the path specified. The APPEND command described in the next section eliminates this restriction.

Each user on the network can create a custom starting file that sets up the path for that particular user. The PATH command for that user must be issued after the user has started the network on his or her system and has initiated his system through the AUTOUSER.BAT file designated for that user.

The APPEND Command

What if you need to load data files that the program must find from another directory? In a network, directory maps can be complex and you may need to create path constructions for data files or overlays, as described in the last section with *WordStar*. To help the network user, IBM added a new DOS external command: APPEND. (Note: The APPEND command is not a part of DOS 3.2. At the present time it is supplied only on the PC Network program disks.) This works just like PATH but applies to *any* type of file, rather than just EXE, COM, and BAT files.

Suppose, for example, in your starting AUTOEXEC.BAT file you add an APPEND \ command. This is a simple way of telling DOS that any time it cannot find *any* file in the current directory it should also check the root directory for the file.

The APPEND command is used to link data files to program files on other directories. For example, if your WS.COM word processor is on a directory called WP along with its overlay files, you could store letters and documents on several directories as LETTERS, MEMOS, and REPORTS. You could then append the WP directory to the current directory, log to the directory with the desired document, and start the word processor. The word processor and all overlay files would properly load, permitting you to edit in the current directory.

Each time you issue a new APPEND command, the previous APPEND is canceled. To cancel all APPEND commands, issue the command:

```
APPEND ;
```

The APPEND command does not work with all application programs. Its effectiveness depends upon how the application program was written. Use caution in selecting your application programs and in installing them for network use. You may find certain programs have constraints when used with *PC Network* or the APPEND command.

The JOIN Command

The DOS JOIN command can be used to logically join two directories to make them appear as one directory structure. The directories are never physically connected, but only appear so to programs and other DOS commands. The directory to be joined must be empty at the time the command is issued. For example, the command:

```
C > JOIN A: C: \ WP   < Enter >
```

logically connects the directory on Drive A to the C: directory. The A: \ directory must be empty (no files). If you use the directory on Drive C after the command you will see the following structure:

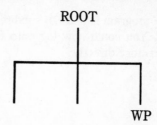

ROOT

WP

where WP appears as a new directory on Drive C.
Several restrictions apply:

1. The root directory on the joined drive must be empty before the command is issued. In this example, there must be no files on the disk in Drive A.

2. You cannot issue the command from the directory to be joined. For example, the following is invalid:

   A> JOIN A: C: \ WP

3. Once you have joined a drive, it becomes invalid as a drive until the join is removed. For example, once you have joined Drive A as C: \ WP, there is no longer a Drive A on the system.

You can delete a JOIN with the /D parameter:

   C > JOIN A: /D < Enter >

At any time, you can display the current JOIN configuration using the JOIN command without a parameter:

   C > JOIN < Enter >

The SUBST Command

This command is the exact converse of JOIN. It lets you separate a directory into two or more logical directories. Using this command, you can assign a drive designator for a path. This is useful for simplifying long path names in command lines. For example, suppose we use the command:

C > SUBST G: C: \ APPS \ DB < Enter >

This assumes our *dBASE* program is in a DB subdirectory within the APPS subdirectory on Drive C. You could now log onto Drive G and execute a program in the APPS directory directly:

C > G: < Enter >
G > DBASE < Enter >

The PERMIT Command

The PERMIT command lets a workstation that is not a server offer disk resources to another user on the network. The command will be discussed in more detail in Chapter 15; for now it is only necessary to see it as a convenient means for any workstation on the network to offer a directory, in effect becoming a temporary server. The disadvantage is that once the command is issued, the machine that issues the command is a 100-percent dedicated server and is no longer a workstation. The second limitation is that only one workstation can use the server resource at a time.

THE "LOST" COMMANDS

Once you start the network some of the DOS commands are no longer available to a user, or function differently. The following commands are affected in a network environment:

CHKDSK.COM	DISKCOPY.COM
FDISK.COM	DISKCOMP.COM
FORMAT.COM	RECOVER.COM
SYS.COM	VERIFY.COM
PRINT.COM	

Each of these either will not work or works differently in the *PC LAN* environment. Most of these commands reference the disk as a physical unit by track and sector. Once the network is started, the disk is only accessible through the network functions as a logical unit. A new print command exists as a part of *PC LAN*: NET PRINT.

If you wish to use CHKDSK to check a hard disk occasionally (which is a good idea), put the command in the AUTOEXEC.BAT file that starts the system and execute it before starting the network.

You will also find, on a server in a *PC LAN* environment, that if the printer is shared you can no longer use Ctrl/PrtSc to print to the printer (Ctrl/P

```
: *** Network Batch File ***
: ***
ECHO OFF
PATH C:\NETWORK
YNPROMPT Y N 39 Do you want to start the network (Y/N)?
IF ERRORLEVEL 1 GOTO A
ECHO ON
NET START SRV SERVER /SRV:5 /SHR:10 /SES:18
NET SHARE DATA = D:\
NET SHARE PRINTER = LPT1
ECHO OFF
GOTO B
:A
PATH \
:B
ECHO ON
AUTOUSER.BAT
```

Fig. 8-1. AUTOEXEC.BAT file created by PC Local Area Network Program.

will not work either). You will also not be able to use Shift/PrtSc to dump the screen. The printer becomes a logical device and is no longer directly accessible, even if the printer is not shared.

STARTING DOS

In a single-user DOS system that is not part of a network, an AUTOEXEC.BAT file can be created that automatically starts the system on booting and executes any start-up commands of interest, such as setting the clock. If AUTOEXEC.BAT exists, DOS automatically finds this file on starting and executes it.

In a system that runs under the *PC Local Area Network* environment, the AUTOEXEC.BAT file serves a completely different purpose: that of starting the network software on the server or workstation.

Let us see how this works. The first time you start your system with the network software you will use your old AUTOEXEC.BAT file as you normally do. Then you will use the NET command with the menu or the NET START command to define the network configuration (see Chapter 11). Once you have defined the configuration, you can request it to be saved. Saving the configuration creates a new AUTOEXEC.BAT file that will automatically start

Fig. 8-2. AUTOUSER.BAT file automatically created from old AUTOEXEC.BAT file.

```
PWRUPCLK
VERIFY ON
CHKDSK
CLS
PROMPT $p$g
```

```
: *** Network Batch File ***
VERIFY ON
CHKDSK
PATH C:\;C:\NETWORK
TOKREUI
NETBEUI
: ***
ECHO OFF
PATH C:\NETWORK
YNPROMPT Y N 39 Do you want to start the network (Y/N)?
IF ERRORLEVEL 1 GOTO A
ECHO ON
NET START SRV SERVER /SRV:5 /SHR:10 /SES:18
NET SHARE DATA=D:\
NET SHARE PRINTER=LPT1
ECHO OFF
GOTO B
:A
PATH \
:B
ECHO ON
AUTOUSER.BAT
```

Fig. 8-3. Modified AUTOEXEC.BAT file.

the system with the same configuration (Fig. 8-1). In this way you do not have to go through the menu or the NET START command each time to start the system.

The next question is, what happens to your old AUTOEXEC.BAT file? You probably have a lot of good commands saved there that you wish executed on starting. *PC LAN* makes provision for this. When you save the network configuration, the old AUTOEXEC.BAT file is saved as an AUTOUSER.BAT file. The AUTOUSER.BAT file will contain all your old start-up commands (Fig. 8-2). Whenever you save the network configuration, the network creates a set of commands that can recreate this configuration, as well as a command to call this AUTOUSER.BAT file and execute it.

There are, therefore, two batch files that are executed automatically on starting. AUTOEXEC.BAT is executed first. It starts and configures the network, and can be modified any time you wish to change the network configuration. After executing, it calls AUTOUSER.BAT. This completes the start-up, setting the clock, path, and other start-up parameters.

If you wish to add special commands on starting that do not work in a network environment, add these to the beginning of the new AUTOEXEC.BAT file after the first line. You should, of course, always add the two resident programs TOKREUI and NETBEUI (see Chapter 11). You may wish to add CHKDSK and VERIFY ON at the beginning of the new AUTOEXEC.BAT file (See Fig. 8-3). Be sure to remove calls to non-network programs (such as VERIFY) from the AUTOUSER.BAT file before rebooting the network.

Chapter 9

Installing the Network: Adapter Testing and Cabling

ONCE THE PLANNING HAS BEEN COMPLETED AND ALL HARDWARE AND software is available, you can then begin the actual installation.

Before you start, however, be sure you have everything you will need to install the network. Read through this and the next chapter completely before beginning, so that you are thoroughly familiar with the procedure. Make a quick check for preparation using the following list:

1. Be sure you have a plan. This should include maps of the network and cabling, documentation of what public and private subdirectories you wish to install on the disk, and any project charts designating who will do what, and when.

2. Be sure each workstation and server is working before continuing. If necessary, install DOS 3.20 on each system and make certain each will boot with the new DOS.

3. Back up all hard disks on all systems.

4. Study your documentation so you are familiar with the steps involved.

5. Involve the users in the installation. Start your training program early.

THE MULTISTATION ACCESS UNIT

Before you can use the MAU, you must first go through a short set-up step with the MAU using the Set-up Aid that comes with the unit. Be sure no cables are connected to the MAU, then plug the Set-up Aid into the slot marked with number 1. The lamp on the aid will glow brightly for a moment, then go out. After about 4 seconds, you will hear a faint click from inside the MAU. Remove the aid, put it in the second slot, and wait 4 seconds again until the light goes out and the faint click is heard. Continue with all eight numeric slots on the MAU. When you have completed all eight, put the aid into the receptacle marked RI for 4 seconds. The light should glow brightly and not go out. The MAU is now ready to use. Save the Set-up Aid. You must use it again if you relocate the MAU. The Set-up Aid contains a battery and should not be put in a fire or be short-circuited.

THE LAN ADAPTER CARD

The LAN Adapter card is easy to install and involves three steps: setting the switches, installing the card, and testing the card.

Setting the Switches

The LAN Adapter card has a single switch on it that determines the interrupt level it will use. Understanding the concept of interrupt levels is not really important for installing the network, but how this switch is set is important. Normally you will use interrupt level two, and when you unpack your card you will probably find the switch already set correctly for this interrupt level.

The IBM PC XT computer supports nine hardware interrupts: parity and eight others (the AT supports several more). Here is the table for the PC XT:

0	Timer
1	Keyboard
2	(reserved)
3	COM2
4	COM1
5	Hard disk
6	Floppy disk
7	Printer

Although the LAN Adapter card normally uses interrupt level 2, you may find that this interrupt level is already in use in your system. In my system, for example, this interrupt is used by a Microsoft mouse. Check your system to be sure this interrupt level is not in use by checking other adapter cards and the documentation for these cards. If you find another device using this same interrupt, try to change the interrupt level on the other device. With a heavily loaded system, you may have trouble finding enough interrupt levels to use all the peripherals. The second interrupt level also may be used by other network adapter cards or special interface cards for remote systems. You may also have problems if you are using an extended memory or an EGA card, particularly if both are in your system.

Be sure computer power is off and the power cord disconnected. Open the cabinet of your computer and examine the system for an available slot. The LAN Adapter card can be installed into any long slot of the XT or AT. It is preferable to install it on an outside slot, because during the installation you may need to move cards around to test the system and outside slots are easier to use. If an outside slot is not available use any free slot. You can put up to two adapters in an IBM XT or IBM AT. If you have an extension unit the adapter card should not be installed in it.

If you have an IBM PC, the card should be installed in slot 4 so it will have adequate ventilation. If another card is in this slot, move it (if at all possible) and use slot 4 for the LAN Adapter card. Only one adapter card should be installed in an IBM PC because of the ventilation requirement.

Check the switches that control the interrupt levels on other cards, and change the switch on the LAN Adapter card that controls the interrupt level if necessary.

Installing and Testing the Card

Now, with the computer off and no power cord connected, use a screwdriver to remove the metal strip that covers the hole on the rear panel near the slot you wish to use. Keep the screw that held the strip in place—you will need it later. You may need to temporarily loosen screws for adjacent cards in order to remove the strip. Be careful that you do not drop the screws onto the system board. If you do drop a screw, carefully remove additional cards and recover any dropped screw.

There should also be a plastic card support that is used to hold the card in place on the end of the card slot opposite the metal strip. If this plastic support is not there, install the plastic card support that comes with the adapter.

Insert the adapter card carefully, being sure the component side faces the same direction as the other adapter cards. Secure it with the screw that was used to hold the metal strip in place. Be sure it is properly seated. Be sure no boards are touching and nothing has fallen on the system board. Tighten all screws. Again, be careful that you do not drop a screw onto the system board. The only thing that should show through the rear of the computer is the DB-9 connector. Keep the metal strip in a safe place in case it is needed again. Label the DB-9 connector as your LAN connector. This prevents confusing it with a mouse or other peripheral connector. Double check again to be sure there are no loose screws on the system board. While the system is open, clean out any loose dust, particularly around the fan.

For the time being keep the card accessible. Either leave the cabinet off for the first tests and be careful the cat and kids do not get into it, or put the cabinet in place and temporarily secure it with one screw. Connect the keyboard, video and power cable.

Now we need to test the card. The disk that came with your LAN Adapter card contains a small diagnostic program. Place this disk in the floppy disk drive and turn the computer on. Boot the system from the diagnostic disk. Locate a network cable and plug the end with the DB-9 plug into the LAN Adapter socket. Leave the other end free—do not plug it into the MAU.

When the system boots from the diagnostic disk, the POST diagnostics should run, then the first menu should appear. Select option 0: "Run diagnostic routines."

From the displayed submenus select the proper options to run the test one time. Select the type of cable from the menu, then start the test. The test should run for a few minutes, then display a message that it completed normally. Note: If the test fails, see the section in this chapter on LAN Adapter Troubleshooting.

Continue your installation with the next system, using the same procedures. Be careful and do not rush your work or try to install the system if you are tired. Continue in this way until an adapter card is installed and tested on each computer.

LAN Adapter Troubleshooting

If the diagnostics do not run on any system, you will see an error message displayed. Use the manual that came with the LAN Adapter Card to resolve the difficulty. Here are some additional guidelines:

1. Be sure your ROM in the computer will function with the network. With a Compaq, you should have Revision F or later. With an IBM, any ROM dated no earlier than November, 1982, will work.

2. Try swapping adapter cards and cables to isolate the problem as much as possible. *Be sure to turn the computer off before swapping cards.* Change only one variable at a time.

3. Check to be sure there are no interrupt conflicts. If the LAN Adapter card is using interrupt level 2, nothing else should use this level.

4. Remove any non-IBM cards or unusual peripherals from the system temporarily to isolate the problem and make the system as completely IBM as possible for the test.

5. Be sure the cables are firmly seated in the adapter sockets and the other end is *not* connected to the MAU.

BUILDING A PROTOTYPE SYSTEM

You can now begin testing the network using a prototype system. For the first setup, use two of the computers (one should have a hard disk), a MAU, and two cables. Connect each of the two systems to the MAU with the cables (Fig. 9-1).

The prototype testing can be done while the cable is being installed, as the prototyping does not use the actual system cable.

Eventually you should check each network component thoroughly using the prototype network before committing the network to your installed wiring. If you experience trouble in this prototype setup, you will find it much easier to move components (cards, MAUs, cables, etc.) around to locate the trouble than by trying to chase problems through cables in the wall. You should check out every computer, adapter card, and MAU with the network before using the installed cables with the network. In other words, complete the steps in this chapter and each succeeding chapter through Chapter 13, using two computers at a time in a test configuration, before starting to use the installed cable.

INSTALLING THE CABLE

Begin the cable installation, following the instructions in Chapter 4. Even though the installed cable is not used at this time, you should begin installing

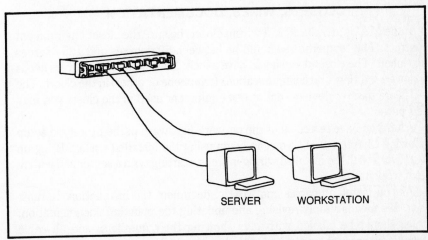

Fig. 9-1. Setting up the prototype system. Courtesy of International Business Machines Corporation.

it. Note: MAUs are a part of the cable system and also used in the prototype setup. Test each multistation access unit before it is finally installed in its final location. As you do your wiring, keep the MAU units temporarily loose (unscrewed) until each MAU has been tested. You will be moving the MAUs occasionally from their wiring closets (or wherever you wish to put them) to your test bed and back again. Once all the prototyping is completed, you can screw the MAUs in place at their permanent locations and add your connectors.

Although the cable carries only small voltages, you should check with your local government to find out if there are any regulations for cabling in your building. In some locations local codes may require placing the cable in conduit. This is particularly true if the cable must pass through a wall that is designed as a fire barrier. You may also need a permit or a licensed contractor.

When you complete your wiring, be sure the MAUs are connected in a ring. The ring-out connector of each must be connected to the ring-in connector of the next in the loop. With one MAU, the network will still work without this jumper, but adding the jumper gains you some fault protection in case of network errors.

When installing the cable, use caution that you do not kink it. Lay the cable in trays or channels. You should not pull the cable through a wall. Bends (even a temporary bend) should be limited to a minimum radius of an inch for standard indoor Type 1 cable. Do not try to reuse old cable, because repeated bending in a small radius can break the internal copper conductors.

IBM provides extensive documentation for installing the cable, and a wide range of support hardware, for a variety of environments. You may wish to enlist the support of a professional installer.

CLOSETS, WIRES, DOCUMENTATION

If the MAUs are placed in a wiring closet, be sure the closet environment is correct. The temperature should be between 50 degrees and 105 degrees Fahrenheit. The closet door should have a lock. You should also address needs for power, lighting, and communications (telephone or other) in the closet. The MAUs are passive devices, but to test equipment used in the closet you may need power.

After you have tested all of the network hardware in the prototype setup (following Chapters 9-13), you can begin using the installed wiring. Bring up the network with the installed wiring in steps, starting with a server and adding a few workstations.

As you install all cables and MAUs, document the installation. In most cases, this means simply revising and updating the planning documentation. Cables should be labeled with tags showing their numbers, and all cable information entered into a log. The log should be a part of the network notebook, and updated whenever the wiring is changed.

Chapter 10

Installing the Network: Names and Directories

B EFORE STARTING THE NETWORK, YOU MUST DEFINE NAMES USED ON the network and create any new directories that will be needed. The *PC Local Area Network* software must then be installed on the proper directory.

ASSIGNING NAMES

There are three types of names used in the *PC LAN* program: session names, private directory names, and network names. Understanding each of these types and the relationships among them is important in understanding how the network functions. The concepts here differ somewhat from those in the *PC Local Area Network* manual. The manual uses the concept of network name to refer to both the session and network name.

Session Names

Each server and workstation is assigned a name on the network. The name serves to identify the computer or workstation to others on the network. A server should be identified by a name that identifies the machine or server function: SERVER1, GRAPHICS, etc. Workstations, in contrast, are identified by a session name that identifies the user: JOHNS, SANDY T, etc.

A user can enter the network from any available workstation and start the network software with any particular session name. Once the session is started that workstation is identified on the network by the session name used in starting up. JOHN and SANDY could each use the same workstation at different times, using their own name as the session name each time they start the network. If John were using the workstation under JOHN and quit, Sandy would need to reboot the workstation and start the network under SANDY for her name to be the session name.

To prevent confusion, we will call the name assigned to a computer (server or workstation) at a particular time as the *session name,* as it refers to a specific user session from a workstation or the server name.

At a workstation, the session name is used for sending messages to other workstations or servers on the network, or to identify the user's workstation to others that may wish to send a message to the user. At the server, in addition to using the session name for the sending and receiving of messages, the session name is used to identify shared server resources on the network.

Your test configuration should have two systems, one of which will be a server. Label the server SERVER1 (or use any other name you prefer) with some tape. Label the second system (which should be a workstation) with the name of a user who will use that workstation.

Private Subdirectory Names

You will want to create a private subdirectory on a server for each user using that server. The private directories are named and created with the Installation Aid when you are installing the *PC LAN* program on the server, but the names are not made available to the users. You can add other private subdirectories without the use of the Installation Aid. In other words, although the private subdirectory will be used by the users, it is not necessary for the user to know the name of the subdirectory.

There is nothing on a server disk that distinguishes a private subdirectory from any other directory. The directory is private in the sense that the name is not known to other users and other users cannot access the disk directory structure.

Network Names

Although each user has a private subdirectory on a server, the name of this private directory is not directly available to the user. The server operator makes it available to a user by offering to share it using the NET SHARE command and then assigning a *network name* to the resource. The network name is also called the short name. Network users can access the subdirectory through the network name (short name).

For example, you may have a private subdirectory on the server called USER01. Using the server's NET SHARE command, the server operator may assign the network (short) name SANDY to this resource. Network users can then request use of this resource (directory) as SANDY. Until the server's NET

SHARE command is issued for this assignment the resource would not be available to anyone on the network, including Sandy. Sandy's workstation or session name may be SANDYT (Fig. 10-1). The only reason the directory is considered private is because the network name (SANDY) is secret, or a password was assigned.

INSTALLING THE PC LAN SOFTWARE

Using the prototype setup, begin the installation of the network on two computers. One computer should be the system you intend to use as a server, the other should be one of the workstations. You can install the workstations and servers in any order. The workstation, however, is easier to install. For this reason, start your installation with the workstation in your test bed (the prototype system).

There are three steps to perform on each system before using it on the network. For a server these are *installing* (Chapters 9-10), *starting* (Chapter 11), and *sharing* (Chapter 12). For the workstation these are installing, starting, and *using* (Chapter 13). The systems can be installed and started in any order. The sharing step, however, must be completed on the server before a workstation can use the shared resource. Remember: Install and start in any order, but share before using.

Installing a Diskette-Based Workstation

If the workstation does not have a hard disk, you must create a disk that contains DOS and the network software.

1. Insert your DOS 3.2 diskette in Drive A and boot your system.

2. Create a new DOS diskette by putting a blank disk in Drive B and formatting it to include the system, using:

FORMAT B:/s < Enter >

Label this disk DOS NET.

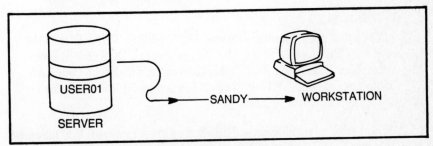

Fig. 10-1. A server resource is offered under a network name.

3. Format two additional disks but don't install the DOS on either. Label one PC NET, label the second MESSAGE MANAGER FOR TOPVIEW. The directions in the manual that comes with *PC LAN* will create two floppy disks: one is a DOS disk for bringing up the network, the second is for using *Topview*. You will quickly discover, however, that if you are using an IBM PC (or a 360K disk drive) the network will not fit on a disk with all the startup files. With an IBM PC or 360K disk drive, then, your final goal is three disks:

DOS NET—The disk with the DOS system, the AUTOEXEC.BAT file, CONFIG.SYS, AUTOUSER.BAT, and the two resident programs TOKREUI.COM and NETBEUI.COM.

PC NET—The disk to bring up the network with all the *PC Local Area Network* software.

MESSAGE MANAGER FOR TOPVIEW—*Topview* disk

4. Remove the master DOS disk from Drive A and insert the master *PC LAN* program disk. Put the new DOS NET disk in Drive B. Enter the following:

A > INSTALL B: ds tvmsg < Enter >

Use ds if Drive B is double-sided double-density (360K). Use hc if the drive is a high-capacity drive (1.2M) such as used on an IBM AT. The hc option forces the program to create a NETWORK subdirectory and copy the programs to that subdirectory. The installation program copies the network software to your new DOS drive and creates a CONFIG.SYS file.

5. Modify the CONFIG.SYS file to contain the following statements:

```
FILES = 20
BUFFERS = 24
LASTDRIVE = N
FCBS = 16,8
STACKS = 64,128
```

6. Depending upon your diskette size, either add the TOKREUI.COM and NETBEUI.COM files to this disk or create a DOS diskette with these files. The TOKREUI.COM file came on a disk with your *LAN* adapter card. The NETBEUI.COM file is on a NETBIOS disk that must be purchased separately.

You now have a bootable network diskette for your system. You may wish to modify the CONFIG.SYS file for any special system requirements. The

COMMAND.COM file that DOS needs is already on this diskette, but the disk contains none of the files that support the external DOS commands, such as CHKDSK. You may wish to copy a few of these external commands to your new system diskette, but use caution. Save plenty of working space on the disk. In addition, it is not really necessary to have too many of the DOS external files on the disk, because you will be able to access all the DOS files on the server disk.

If you are using an IBM PC, all the files to boot the system and start the network will not fit on a 360K diskette. Create one diskette as the DOS boot disk with an AUTOEXEC.BAT file that starts TOKREUI and NETBEUI. It should also contain the CONFIG.SYS file created by the above installation procedure. Put your network software (the disk you created in the previous steps) on a second disk. Use this second disk to start the network after booting.

Installing a Hard-Disk Workstation

If you have a workstation that includes a hard disk, first be sure the hard disk is backed up. Install the network software to the hard disk by putting the network software disk in Drive A and entering:

INSTALL C: HC < Enter >

Be sure to use the correct hard disk designator. This will create a NETWORK subdirectory on the hard disk and copy all the network files to that subdirectory. The CONFIG.SYS file, if it existed, will be modified.

You may still need to edit the CONFIG.SYS file after installation. Modify the CONFIG.SYS file to include the following lines if they are not there:

FILES = 20
BUFFERS = 24
LASTDRIVE = N
FCBS = 16,8
STACKS = 64,128

You will also need to transfer the TOKREUI.COM and NETBEUI.COM programs to the hard disk from their respective floppy disks.

Installing PC LAN on a Server

Installing the *PC Local Area Network Program* on a server is considerably more complex than installing the software on a workstation. The reason is that public and private areas on the disk must be defined, and programs that are to be accessed by the users must be moved to a public area. Fortunately, IBM supplies an Installation Aid that creates the necessary subdirectories.

You don't have to use the Installation Aid to initialize a server or create the special server directories be used with *PC LAN*. The installation procedure is simply a method that will help you organize and manage the server resources effectively. If you wish, test the network with your prototype and gain some experience on how the various types of names work. Once you have learned a few things you can configure the disk, load the network software to a NETWORK subdirectory and add access to this directory to your current path. In either case, be sure to add the TOKREUI.COM and NETBEUI.COM programs to the root directory. With or without the Installation Aid, once the software is on the hard disk you can start the network.

The Installation Aid does four tasks:

1. It creates a subdirectory called NETWORK, if it does not already exist, and copies all the network programs to this subdirectory.

2. It creates a public subdirectory called APPS (if it does not already exist) that contains programs available to all users. The programs may be organized into subdirectories within APPS. For example, the DOS programs are in a subdirectory called DOS under APPS. After the installation, you may wish to set all the programs in APPS to read-only that are not already so set by using the ATTRIB command.

3. It creates a private directory for each user you assign to the system. Each private subdirectory contains a BATCH subdirectory under it which will contain the private batch files that the user needs to start the programs in APPS.

4. Automatically creates the necessary batch files for each user in the BATCH subdirectory of their private area and also creates a BATCH subdirectory from the main root that contains the batch files for starting programs from the server.

As you can imagine, installing the server involves a major reorganization of the disk. You should take the time to make a complete backup of the hard disk before starting.

If you have been using a version of DOS 2.0 with a hard disk of 20 megabytes or more, you should reformat the disk after backing it up and before using the Installation Aid. This will create a new File Allocation Table (FAT) that makes more efficient use of the disk space than your older DOS 2.0. DOS 3.2 permits a hard disk of 20 megabytes or more to save files using a minimum of 2K space.

If you already have files and directories on the disk, you can use the Installation Aid to add the new directories if there is sufficient room.

A map of a typical network server directory after *PC Network* installation is shown in Fig. 10-2. The corresponding file map is shown in Fig. 10-3.

Public files are stored in an APPS subdirectory. This public directory has a tree-like structure in which application programs are grouped in appropriate subdirectories under APPS. There is also a private subdirectory under the root for each user, with a BATCH subdirectory under each private subdirectory. The network software is in a NETWORK subdirectory, and the batch files for the server are in a BATCH subdirectory. Here is a general overview of each directory:

ROOT—Contains the minimum DOS files to start DOS: CONFIG.SYS, TOKREUI.COM, NETBEUI.COM, AUTOEXEC.BAT, and AUTOUSER.BAT.

NETWORK—Contains *PC LAN* programs used by the server. They are not available to users.

APPS—This is the public directory for all users. It contains application programs (network versions), network programs, and batch files used by everyone on the network. Each collection of programs is in a subdirectory under APPS (DOS, NETWORK, etc.). All programs are set to a read-only status.

USER Subdirectories—These have the name of each user, and are accessible only by the users. The PROFILE subdirectory contains programs and data files used by the individual user. The BATCH subdirectory contains the user's batch files.

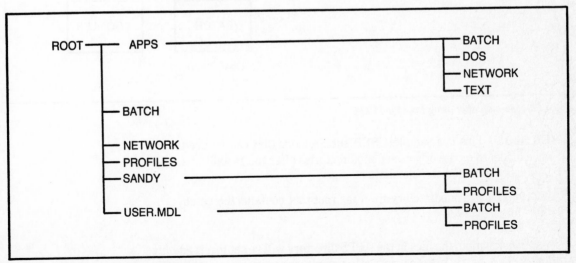

Fig. 10-2. Directory map after installation.

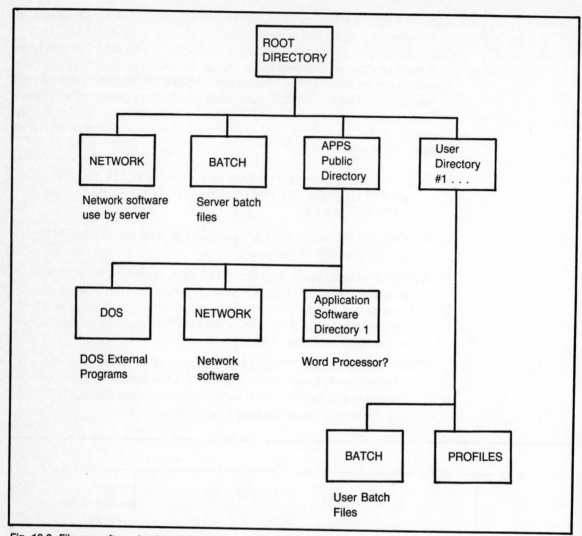

Fig. 10-3. File map after using Installation Aid.

USER.MDL—This is a sample USER subdirectory that can be used as a model to create other user subdirectories after the Installation Aid has completed the installation.

BATCH—This is a subdirectory from the root that contains the batch files for the server.

After installation, the files in the APPS directory will be set to a read-only attribute. This is to prevent network users from erasing a public file inadvertently. You would not, for example, want a user to try to edit the COMMAND.COM file with a word processor (no kidding—it has happened). If you ever wish to delete any of these files, you would need to change the read attribute with the ATTRIB command.

Notice that the Installation Aid does some duplication of the DOS and network programs on the server. This duplication is not really necessary for most networks. For example, if the DOS files and network software will not be on the local workstations, they must be available in appropriate subdirectories on the server APPS subdirectory. If the network software is in an \APPS\NETWORK subdirectory, there is no need for it to also be in a NETWORK subdirectory. The COMMAND.COM file of DOS must be in the root directory in order to boot the server, but the remainder of the DOS files can be accessed from APPS/DOS.

Before starting the Installation Aid you should collect the information you will need for the program. This will save you trying to pull it together as the program is executing. You should also create a copy of the Installation Aid disk that came with your *PC LAN* software. Once you are ready, here is what you will need to install with the Installation Aid:

1. The session name for the server (such as SERVER1). This will be used by the system when messages are sent or received.

2. The name for each user private subdirectory. Each workstation has a name in the network that designates the current session. Any user may use the public subdirectory, whether or not he or she has a private directory. What you need to define at this time is the name that will be assigned to each private subdirectory. This is *not* the same as the session or server name that will be used for messages.

3. The names of all the IBM application programs you wish to install in APPS. You will find a quick list to choose from in the *Installation Aid Quick Reference* in the back of the *PC Local Area Network User's Guide*. Later you will want to add other non-IBM application programs to this subdirectory. Note: You cannot use the Installation Aid to add non-IBM programs to the APPS subdirectory.

4. A copy of the Installation Aid disk.

If you wish to create your own directory structure, study Figs. 10-2 and 10-3; then map your own structure. The basic concept to remember is that the major factor that slows DOS down is too many file entries in a single subdirectory. Each buffer in use can hold 16 directory entries. If you have 24 buffers (BUFFERS = 24) in CONFIG.SYS, you can keep approximately 384 directory file entries in memory. If a directory size exceeds this, DOS will slow down dramatically, since it uses a sequential search on the directory. Search time will increase exponentially with the number of clusters in use. If you have to use a large number of files in a directory, increase the value for BUFFERS in CONFIG.SYS to 99. This will permit up to approximately 1400 files in a directory without speed degradation.

If possible, you should start with an empty directory on the hard disk. If you wish, you can even use the Installation Aid to install DOS to an empty (but formatted) hard disk. This will prevent you from confusing subdirectories and files created by the Installation Aid with data already on the disk.

If the hard disk is completely empty (no DOS), boot the system from a DOS system disk in the diskette drive. If the hard disk has DOS on it, boot from the hard disk. Put the copy of the Installation Aid disk in the drive. Select the drive with the disk and enter:

A > G   < Enter >

The program will start and display the main menu (Fig. 10-4). Select the first

```
                    IBM PC Local Area Network Program Installation Aid

                              MAIN MENU

          Choose one of the following:

          1.   Install DOS, IBM PC LAN Program and other IBM applications

          2.   Name the network users who can use your applications

          3.   Display information about your installed applications

          4.   Display how network users can use your applications

          __ Choice




          Enter - Continue
          Esc - Exit
                                                        F1 - Help
```

Fig. 10-4. Main Installation Aid menu.

option. The Installation Aid will then do some disk work (creating the APPS directory), and you will see the Installing Applications menu (Fig. 10-5).

If the disk does not have DOS installed, install DOS first. The program will ask for the DOS disks as they are needed. Be sure to use DOS 3.2 or later.

Once DOS is installed, select the second option to install the *PC Local Area Network Program*. You will then be asked for the session name you assign to the server. Enter the desired session name, such as SERVER1.

You are then asked for a drive designator. This is the designator you wish the user to assign to the public directory. Although it has no real effect from the server's perspective, this designator is used to create some batch files for each user that will use the public directory. Use K, L, M, or N. Enter the appropriate directory. For example, you could use K for the first server, L for the second, etc. Insert the *PC LAN Program* disk when the Installation Aid asks for this disk.

If you plan to use any IBM application software, you should install this next. Select the programs individually from the menu, and the aid will guide you through each installation. You cannot use this option to install non-IBM

```
         IBM PC Local Area Network Program Installation Aid

                      INSTALLING APPLICATIONS

   and   to choose the application you want to install


  _____ Top of List _____

  DOS
  IBM PC Local Area Network Program
  _____

  Asynchronous Communications (2.00)
  BASIC Compiler (1.00)
  COBOL Compiler (1.00)
  Computers and Communications (1.00)
  DisplayWrite Legal Support (1.00)
  DisplayWrite Medical Support (1.00)
  DisplayWrite 1 (1.00)
  DisplayWrite 3 (1.10)



  Enter - Continue                         PgUp and PgDn - Scroll list
  Esc - Previous Screen                    F1 - Help
```

Fig. 10-5. Option 1 menu.

programs such as *dBASE III* or Microsoft *Word.* These must be installed later on APPS without the Installation Aid. When each program is installed, the aid does the following:

1. Copies the program to the APPS subdirectory, creating any subdirectories under APPS to support the application as needed by the application.

2. It creates two forms of the batch file to start each program. One will be for users, stored in each user private subdirectory. The second form is for starting the program on the server, saved in a BATCH subdirectory created under the main root directory. Note: It is suggested that you install at least one IBM application program at this time. This will give you some idea of the types of files created for application software and where they are created. These can then be used as a model for installing non-IBM application software.

Finally, exit this menu and return to the main menu. Select the second option on the main menu to enter the "user names." The option is confusing, but the intent is *not* to enter the session names, but to assign names to the *private* directories on the disk during installation. For example, if you enter GEORGE, when the installation is complete you will see a new subdirectory called GEORGE.

After each subdirectory is installed, you will get the message "XXX will be able to use applications," which implies a user can now use the public directory. The message is misleading, because the name displayed is actually the name of the private subdirectory (rather than the user session name), and the public subdirectory can be used regardless of whether or not a user has a private subdirectory.

The third option prints a report for the server. This should be saved as a record of the installation in a notebook for the administrator (Fig. 10-6).

The fourth option prints a report for each user, showing the subdirectory name used for the installation (Fig. 10-7). In reality, however, this report should not be distributed to users, as the user never uses or needs the name of the private subdirectory. This report, as the last, should be saved in the administrator's notebook.

COMPLETING THE INSTALLATION

Once you have completed the use of the Installation Aid, take the time to do some clean-up work with the installation. Here are some other things to check:

1. The DOS files are in a DOS subdirectory within the public APPS directory. Is this where you want them (so workstations can use

```
--------------------------------------------------------------------

PLEASE GIVE THIS INFORMATION TO:  SERVER1
Follow these instructions to share your directories with the network

IF YOU'RE USING MENUS, DO THESE STEPS:

1.  You should be following the instructions in the IBM PC Local Area Network
    Program manual.  You should already have:
        a.  Read Chapter 1.
        b.  Read and followed the instructions in Chapter 2.
        c.  Read Chapter 3.

    You should be in Chapter 4 and have started the IBM PC Local Area Network
    Program on your computer.  You should be following the instructions for
    "Setting Up the IBM PC Local Area Network Program for Your Computer."

2.  You need to start sharing your applications directory so that
    other users on the network can use your applications.  Use this
    information to complete the menus:

        DOS name for directory:  C:\APPS
        Network Name of disk or directory: APPS
        Password:  (leave this blank)
        Other users can:  (choose 1)

3.  You also need to start sharing the private directories for each of
    the other users.  Use this information to complete the menus,
    then continue with the instructions in Chapter 4.


--------------------------------------------------------------------

Share information for remote user named: SANDY

        DOS name for directory:            C:\SANDY

        Network name for your directory:   SANDY

        Password for directory (Optional):  your-choice
  NOTE: If you provide a password on this screen, you must also tell
        the corresponding remote user the password.

        Enter the number 5 to choose READ/WRITE/CREATE/DELETE
```

Fig. 10-6. Server report.

them), or do you wish them to be local to the server only? Move if necessary.

2. The network software is in two places: in a NETWORK subdirectory under the root and in a NETWORK subdirectory under the public APPS directory. Do you need them both places? If not, which is appropriate?

```
PLEASE GIVE THIS INFORMATION TO:  SANDY
Follow these instructions to start using applications from SERVER1:


1.  You should be following the instructions in the IBM PC Local Area Network
    Program User's Guide manual.  You should already have:
        a.  Read Chapter 1.
        b.  Read and followed the instructions in Chapter 2.
        c.  Read Chapter 3.
    You should be in Chapter 4 and have started the IBM PC Local Area Network
    Program on your computer.  You should be following the instructions for
    "Setting Up the IBM PC Local Area Network Program for Your Computer."

2.  The applications on SERVER1 are installed in a directory named APPS.
    You need to start using the APPS directory so that you can use
    the applications.  Use the following information to complete
    the menus:

        Disk or directory is on computer: SERVER1
        Network Name of disk or directory: APPS
        DOS drive name on your computer for disk or directory: K

3.  SERVER1 also has installed a private directory for you.  You need to
    start using the private directory so that you can use the
    applications from SERVER1.  Use the following information to complete
    the menus:

        Disk or directory is on computer: SERVER1
        Network Name of disk or directory: SANDY
        DOS drive name on your computer for disk or directory: _
                (You choose the letter, from E - N, but don't use K)
        Password: _____  (if the directory has a password, SERVER1
                             must tell you what it is)

4.  Continue with the instructions in Chapter 4.
```

Fig. 10-7. "User" report after installation.

3. You should add a PATH command to your AUTOEXEC file so that the DOS and network files are accessed automatically from any subdirectory.

4. Programs in the APPS directory (and subdirectories under it) should be set to a read-only status. Check this, changing any as necessary using the DOS ATTRIB command.

5. Modify the CONFIG.SYS file, as necessary, to include the following lines:

```
FILES = 20
BUFFERS = 24
LASTDRIVE = N
FCBS = 16,8
STACKS = 64,128
```

6. Be sure the TOKREUI.COM and NETBEUI programs are on the disk root directory.

ADDING NON-IBM APPLICATION PROGRAMS

Once you have completed the Installation Aid, you may wish to add additional programs to the public subdirectory so they are available to other users on the network. These programs may include utilities, compilers, word processors, and more. These must be added manually to the APPS subdirectory.

Adding an application program to this subdirectory does not automatically mean all users can use the program at the same time. For example, adding a word processor to the APPS subdirectory is only realistic if you are using a network version of the word processing program and the program is designed to support users under the APPS subdirectory. Use caution and check with the manufacturer before installing an application program for public use on the network. Most non-network application programs are designed for a single user, and their license specifically limits their use to a single user at a time. Trying to use them with multiple users on a network can cause unpredictable results.

Before starting, find out if the application program uses any special subdirectories and the names of those subdirectories. Sometimes you can find these by using the TREE command on the application program disk as:

```
C:TREE A:    < Enter >
```

You will also need to find the drive name that the Installation Aid assigned to the APPS subdirectory. As a server operator, you can use APPS as a subdirectory. Workstations will see it as an independent drive, normally K or N (whatever you specified with the Installation Aid). You can find this by examining the C:\NETWORK\SYS_IDS.NIA file. This file contains the drive name.

Now you can install your application program:

1. Create a subdirectory under APPS for your program, adding additional subdirectories under it for any subdirectories the program needs.

2. Copy your program to these directories—i.e., add the program as a subdirectory under APPS.

3. Add a batch file for starting the program in each user subdirectory, using the batch files created by the Installation Aid as a model. You

```
                        SYSTEM DESCRIPTION
SYSTEM _____
SERIAL# _____
VENDOR _____
INSTALLATION DATE _____

SLOT# _____
ADAPTER BOARD _____
INTERRUPT LEVEL _____
INSTALLATION DATE _____

SLOT# _____
ADAPATOR BOARD _____
INTERRUPT LEVEL _____
INSTALLATION DATE _____

SLOT# _____
ADAPATOR BOARD _____
INTERRUPT LEVEL _____
INSTALLATION DATE _____

(Add more as appropriate. You may also wish to add warranty information, repair contact, etc.)
```

Fig. 10-8. System description.

will also need to add a batch file in the BATCH subdirectory from the root so you can start the program from the server. In creating these batch files, you will need the drive designator for the APPS subdirectory that was defined earlier. Use existing batch files for IBM application software as a model.

```
                        SOFTWARE PROFILE
NAME _____
VERSION _____
SERIAL NUMBER _____
NETWORK SUPPORT? _____
TYPE _____
MEMORY REQUIRED _____
PURCHASE DATE _____
SPECIAL
REQUIREMENTS _____
_____
_____

VENDOR _____
TELEPHONE # _____
```

Fig. 10-9. Software profiles.

DIRECTORY MAP

SERVER _____

DRIVE DESIGNATOR _____

PUBLIC DIRECTORY   NETWORK NAME   PASSWORD

PRIVATE SUBDIRECTORY   NETWORK NAME   PASSWORD

Fig. 10-10. Directory map.

4. Use the ATTRIB command to set the attribute of the programs to read-only.

DOCUMENTING THE INSTALLATION

Once you have installed the *PC Local Area Network Program,* you should document the installation for yourself, the system administrator, and each user. At the present time you have used the Installation Aid to define the private subdirectories on a server. Define each session name (workstation/user designator) that you will need to use, as well as the network name for each private subdirectory. You also may wish to assign a password for each user (session name). Create a final report for the administrator showing all names, and a report for each user showing the network names and the password available to the user. You should also print a directory map and a catalog of programs in each directory. Print the listings of each batch file and other special files created by the Installation Aid.

A general guideline for some of the documentation is shown in Figs. 10-8 through 10-10. Add additional information as desired.

Chapter 11

Starting the
PC LAN Program

BEFORE STARTING THE NETWORK BE SURE YOU HAVE COMPLETED ALL the installation steps in Chapters 9 and 10. You should still be using your test setup—a simple network comprising two systems, one of which is a server.

Before the network can be used for productive work three processes must be completed: starting the network, allocating resources on the servers, and accepting offered resources on the workstation. This chapter discusses starting the network. The next two describe the sharing and using of resources.

The *PC LAN* software functions as a collection of resident programs on each workstation and server of the network. Resident programs are programs that reside in memory, coexisting with other programs. MODE and PRINT are resident programs that are a part of DOS. *Sidekick* and *Prokey* are examples of commercial resident programs. *PC LAN*, like many other resident programs, is loaded on boot-up and remains in memory while other application programs are executing.

On any computer, the network resident programs may or may not be active at any particular time, but are always present in memory. The disadvantage of this is that the program always take up memory. The advantage is that the network software is only a few keystrokes away at anytime. When you load any application program, such as *dBASE III* or Microsoft *Word,* it is loaded into memory with the network software. There must be enough memory for both to function.

Any computer physically connected to the network can be used independently of the network without the network software being loaded. The computer can be made a part of the network at any time by loading and start-ing the network resident programs.

The *PC LAN* software must be started on each computer that is a part of the network. The process of starting the network on a server or workstation defines three things: the session name; which of the four configurations the computer will use; and parameters that control, or "tune," various aspects of the system.

Remember that the *PC Local Area Network* is a peer-to-peer network. There is no hierarchy. Each station is assigned an identifying name—its session name. Servers are assigned session names that indicate the machine function (such as SERVER1). Workstations are assigned the names of the user. The session name can contain up to 15 characters.

Although a unique session name is assigned to each workstation, there is no way any user can find out who else is on the network (the other session names). There is no directory or list of session names. The administrator must maintain a list of names. If Bob Charleston sat at a workstation and knew how to start it on the network, he could start the network on that machine under any arbitrary name (including his own). A server would have no way of knowing whether or not Bob was a legitimate user. This does not mean, however, that Bob would be able to access resources on the server. Resource access (directories, printers, etc.) is controlled by network names and, optionally, passwords. Bob may get on the network, but he would find that all he could do would be to send messages to another user (assuming he knew the user's session name), unless he knew the network names for the resources.

When a network is started on any server or workstation, the startup program makes a request for the session name that will be assigned to the session. The only check made when the name is entered is to be sure that name is not already assigned to anyone else on the network. There are no passwords or other types of access controls.

Starting *PC LAN* on a computer also requires you to define the configuration. You do not have to know much about the four configurations to do this; the program just asks a few simple questions such as "Share your printer?" From this, *PC LAN* can determine the proper configuration.

Starting the network on a workstation or server assigns a session name to the machine, defines which of the four configurations will be used, and permits the user to set various parameters that tune the network for optimal efficiency.

The *PC Local Area Network Program* can be started in any of three ways:

1. Using the NET command to initiate a menu-driven start procedure.

2. Using the NET START command with the appropriate parameters, bypassing the menu-driven procedures.

3. Using an AUTOEXEC.BAT file, containing a NET START command with the appropriate parameters.

Once the network is started on a computer, the workstation or server can send or receive messages, but no support has yet been initiated to share or use any resources (files, printers, etc.). To share resources, a specific request must be made after the network is started.

If you are starting a server in your test configuration, complete this chapter and the next before starting the workstation. Then return to this chapter and start the workstation, step by step, following which you should turn to Chapter 13 to complete the startup on the workstation. Note: The Installation Aid is normally used on the server to establish the correct directory structure on the hard disk before starting the network.

Before *PC LAN* can be started on a server or workstation, two programs must already be started and resident in memory: TOKREUI and NETBEUI. Be sure these are on the current directory and issue the commands, loading each. The programs must be loaded in this order:

```
C> TOKREUI   <Enter>
C> NETBEUI   <Enter>
```

Once you have started the network the first time and created the AUTOEXEC.BAT batch file, you will want to add the steps to load these two programs to the AUTOEXEC.BAT file.

STARTING THE NETWORK

Let's look at each of the three methods of starting the network. Remember to start servers first. Remember, too, that once you have started your network, there is no way to display the session name, configuration, or parameters. Keep a written record of the information that you enter for your documentation purposes.

The Menu Alternative

The easiest method of starting the network is to use the NET command. This will initiate a menu-driven procedure to start the network.

1. From the DOS prompt, enter NET (be sure you are on the directory that contains this program.) The full-screen IBM logo is displayed. Press <Enter>.

2. The program will request the "network" name (Fig. 11-1). This will be the session name by which your workstation or server is identified

```
                                                      PC LAN PROGRAM

                    Starting the Network

Please type in a network name for your computer
SERVER1_____




Enter - Continue                      F1 - Help
Esc - Exit

```

Fig. 11-1. Entering the session name.

on the system. Enter up to 15 characters and press <Enter>. Examples: SERVER1, SANDYT. The name must not be used by any other server or workstation on the network.

The program then asks a few questions in order to define the desired configuration. The first question determines whether the system will be a server (Fig. 11-2):

Share your printer? disks? directories?

If your answer Y to this, the program assumes the workstation is a messenger and skips to the next step. For most workstations you will answer this affirmatively. If you answer with an N, a final question is displayed:

Add user names, forward messages, and use the network request key?

```
                                                      PC LAN PROGRAM
                    Starting the Network

     Please type in a network name for your computer
     SERVER1

     To start the network you have to choose how you want to use the
     network.   Type Y (Yes) or N (No) for the following and press Enter :


     Y  Share your printer? disks? directories?






     Enter - Continue                  F1 - Help
     Esc - Exit                        Tab - Cursor to next field
```

Fig. 11-2. Choosing how to use the network.

If your answer Y to this, the program assumes the workstation is a messenger and skips to the next step. For most workstations you will answer this affirmatively. If you answer with an N, a final question is displayed:

Receive and save messages?

If you answer this with a Y, the program assumes the workstation to be a receiver; otherwise the workstation is assumed to be a redirector.

3. The screen then asks if you wish to accept the default parameter values (Fig. 11-3):

Change defaults for starting?

For now, answer this with an N. Later you will learn how to use this option to tune your network for maximum efficiency.

```
                                                PC LAN PROGRAM
                    Starting the Network

Please type in a network name for your computer
SERVER1_____

To start the network you have to choose how you want to use the
network.   Type Y (Yes) or N (No) for the following and press Enter :


Y   Share your printer? disks? directories?


N   Change defaults for starting?




Enter - Continue                    F1 - Help
Esc - Exit                          Tab - Cursor to next field
```

Fig. 11-3. Accepting the default settings.

4. A final confirmation screen is displayed (Fig. 11-4). Check the screen, then enter Y to the prompt, and the network will start. You will see a message that the network is starting and hear a few beeps, after which you will be returned to the network program's main menu (Fig. 11-5). The network program is now resident in memory and active.

Starting from the Command Line

You can also start the network from the command prompt, using the NET START command and a minimum of two parameters. The first parameter should be the abbreviation for the desired configuration, the second parameter should define the session name. For example:

C>NET START SRV SERVER1   <Enter>

This starts the computer as a server with the session name SERVER1. The

```
                                                        PC LAN PROGRAM
              Starting the Network   (continued)

   You will be able to do the following:

    Send messages to other computers
    Use network disks, directories, and printers
    Receive messages from other computers
    Allow saving of messages in a save file
    Use the network request key to interrupt your work and use the
     network program
    Receive messages for other names
    Transfer messages to other computers
    Share your disks, directories, and printers


    Y  Do you want to do these tasks?



   Enter - Start the network          F1 - Help
   Esc - Previous menu
```

Fig. 11-4. The final prompt to start the network.

accepted configuration abbreviations are as follows:

SRV	Server
MSG	Messenger
RCV	Receiver
RDR	Redirector

Just as when using the menu to start the network, you can control various startup parameters that relate to the network. Starting from the menu permits you to control up to six parameters. With the NET START command, however, you have access to control of 18 parameters. For the moment you can omit the use of these parameters.

Automatic Start

Going through the menu or using the NET START command each time to start your computer on the network is cumbersome and not necessary. The

```
                                                    PC LAN PROGRAM
            Main Menu - Task Selection

   1. Message tasks

   2. Printer tasks

   3. Disk or directory tasks

   4. Print queue tasks

   5. Network status tasks

   6. Pause and continue tasks

   7. Save or cancel the network setup


   1  Choice

   Enter - Continue                      F1 - Help
   Esc - Exit
```

Fig. 11-5. PC Network server main menu.

menu or NET START is generally used only the first time you start a system on the network, or if you wish to change a startup parameter. After the network is started, you can save the current configuration as a series of commands in an AUTOEXEC.BAT file. After saving the configuration you can use the AUTOEXEC.BAT file to start your computer automatically to the same network configuration each time it is booted.

Saving the configuration is much like taking a picture of your network. All resource allocations, parameter settings and other variables that relate to the network are saved as a series of network commands that permit the user to return to that identical configuration automatically on each bootup.

Note: When a computer is used for a *PC LAN* server or workstation, the AUTOEXEC.BAT file contains only the network startup commands. When the network configuration is saved, commands that previously were in the single-user AUTOEXEC.BAT file are automatically saved in an AUTOUSER.BAT file. The AUTOUSER.BAT file is executed on startup after the AUTOEXEC.BAT file is executed (Fig. 11-6).

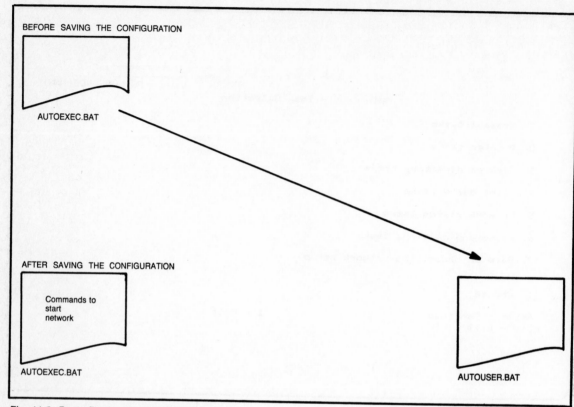

Fig. 11-6. Reconfiguring the AUTOEXEC.BAT file.

SAVING THE CONFIGURATION

You may wish to save your configuration before continuing. If the main menu is not displayed, use the NET or Ctrl/Alt/Break keys to access the main menu (see Fig. 11-5). Select "Save or cancel the network setup." The option menu is then displayed. Select "Save your network setup" (Fig. 11-7). The configuration will be saved and the message "Network, setup saved" displayed. You may wish to examine the AUTOEXEC.BAT file after saving your configuration (Fig. 11-8). You should see a batch file that starts the network with the NET START command. At the end of the file you will see the call to the new AUTOUSER.BAT file. If you already had an AUTOEXEC.BAT file before saving the configuration, it will now be called AUTOUSER.BAT.

Once you have created the AUTOEXEC.BAT file, each time you boot the computer read the commands in this file first to try to start *PC LAN*. The prompt from the AUTOEXEC.BAT batch file will be displayed for the user:

Do you want to start the network (Y/N)?

100

```
                                                  PC LAN PROGRAM
                Save or Cancel Network Setup

   1. Save your network setup

   2. Cancel your current network setup


   1  Choice






   Enter - Continue                    F1 - Help
   Ctrl-Home - Return to Main Menu      Esc - Previous menu
```

Fig. 11-7. Saving the network setup.

If you answer Y, the network will start. Otherwise, the workstation will function as a computer independent of the network and the network software will not be loaded.

```
: *** Network Batch File ***
: ***
ECHO OFF
PATH C:\NETWORK
YNPROMPT Y N 39 Do you want to start the network (Y/N)?
IF ERRORLEVEL 1 GOTO A
ECHO ON
NET START SRV SERVER /SRV:5 /SHR:10 /SES:18
ECHO OFF
GOTO B
:A
PATH \
:B
ECHO ON
AUTOUSER.BAT
```

Fig. 11-8. AUTOEXEC.BAT file after saving the configuration.

Unfortunately, if you try this with your Token-Ring Network at this point you will find it will not work. The software for the Token-Ring adapter card needs to be loaded each time before the network will start. The TOKREUI and NETBEUI commands must be added to the batch file. There are also some other commands that you may wish to execute on startup before the network is started. These should be left in the AUTOEXEC.BAT file before saving the configuration, and will remain at the beginning of the new AUTOEXEC.BAT file created by *PC LAN* after the first line and before the second.

Important Note: Commands added to AUTOEXEC.BAT *must* be placed between the two first lines in the AUTOEXEC.BAT file created by *PC LAN*. If you save the configuration again later, commands placed between these first two "colon" lines will be saved at the same point in the new AUTOEXEC.BAT file. For example, you *must* add the TOKREUI and NETBEUI commands for the network to start properly. Once added the first time at this location, however, these commands will automatically remain in the AUTOEXEC.BAT file at the proper position if the configuration is saved again. In addition, the AUTOUSER file will not be altered and will remain correct through subsequent configuration saves.

Typically, you will want to add commands to switch the verify on and start both TOKREUI and NETBEUI before starting the network, as the VERIFY command is not available after the network is started (Fig. 11-9). You may also wish to add the CHKDSK command before starting the network and any resident programs that you wish to start before the *PC Local Area Network Program.*

If you are using resident programs, you will need to decide for each whether

```
: *** Network Batch File ***
VERIFY ON
TOKREUI
NETBEUI
: ***
ECHO OFF
PATH C:\NETWORK
YNPROMPT Y N 39 Do you want to start the network (Y/N)?
IF ERRORLEVEL 1 GOTO A
ECHO ON
NET START SRV SERVER /SRV:5 /SHR:10 /SES:18
ECHO OFF
GOTO B
:A
PATH \
:B
ECHO ON
AUTOUSER.BAT
```

Fig. 11-9. *AUTOEXEC.BAT file after editing to add TOKREUI and NETBEUI.*

to load it before or after the *PC LAN* programs. To load them before *PC LAN*, add them before the TOKREUI and NETBEUI programs after the first line of the new AUTOEXEC.BAT file. These commands will then stay there, even through subsequent configuration saves. To load a resident program after *PC LAN*, add it to the AUTOUSER.BAT file in the proper place.

USING THE MENUS

Once you have started *PC LAN*, you can execute the network functions in either of two ways: using the main menu or using the command mode. You will probably want to use the menus until you have developed some confidence. Once you are comfortable and you like the convenience of entering the commands directly from the DOS prompt, you can bypass the menus and use commands directly. In the subsequent chapters you will see both methods of executing each function. For the moment, let us look more closely at the menu alternative.

If the DOS prompt is displayed you can always access the *PC Network* main menu with any of the four configurations by typing NET < Return >. When *PC LAN* is not operational (resident), the NET command loads and starts the network. Once you have started the network, this command accesses the main menu. If you are a server or messenger, you can also access the *PC LAN* main menu from within another program or from the DOS prompt by using the Ctrl/Alt/Break keys. A server has a slightly different main menu than the workstation.

Using the Ctrl/Alt/Break keys is much like activating any resident program. When the Ctrl/Alt/Break keys are pressed, the application program remains in suspended memory while the *PC Local Area Network Program* becomes active. You can use the escape key to return to the application program, exactly where you left off. *PC LAN* is always in memory. When you are using application programs, the network redirector acts as a shell on top of DOS, redirecting resource requests from the application program as necessary. *PC LAN* becomes an active program when NET is entered or the Ctrl/Alt/Break keys are pressed.

If you are using *PC LAN* with other resident programs you may find some interaction. Almost all resident programs function by trapping keyboard requests, such as the Ctrl/Alt/Break keys in the case of *PC LAN*. The keyboard request activates the program. Some resident programs can interact with each other. If you do discover a problem, try loading the resident programs in a different order. If you plan to use *Sidekick*, for example, *Sidekick* must be started after *PC Network* is started. The *Sidekick* startup must be in the AUTOUSER.BAT file.

You should note that the Ctrl/Alt/Break keys may not work to start the network program from some programs when the screen is in the graphics mode. Trying to use the Ctrl/Alt/Break keys in this mode may lock up the computer.

On most *PC LAN* option screens, you will find the following active keys:

<Esc>	Returns you to the previous menu. On the main menu, it permits you to exit *PC LAN*.
<Ctrl/Home>	Returns you to the main menu.
<Ctrl/Break>	Exits PC Network.
<Tab>	Move to next menu option.
<Enter>	Completes screen entry.
<F1>	Help screen.
<F2>	Switch to command mode.
<F3>	Change colors on a color monitor.

The following keys are active for editing an option screen:

&longrightarrow;	Move cursor right one character.
&longleftarrow;	Move cursor left one character
<End>	Move cursor to end of line.
<Home>	Move cursor to beginning of line.
<Ctrl/End>	Erase characters to right of cursor.
<Backspace>	Move left and delete character to left of cursor.
<Del>	Delete character.
<Ins>	Toggle insert mode.

STOPPING THE NETWORK

There is no real way to stop the network after it is started except by rebooting the computer. You can use NET PAUSE to temporarily suspend the network, but the program still remains in memory, occupying memory space. There is no way to recover the memory space used by *PC LAN* except by rebooting the computer.

As with a single-user system, you can reboot a computer using the Ctrl/Alt/Del keys. If the network has been started, however, you will get a warning prompt asking if you are sure. You should never reboot a server unless you are sure there are no workstations using the server resources.

RECONFIGURATION AND STARTUP PARAMETERS

PC LAN has 18 parameters that can be used to control the efficiency of the network. You can "tune" the network by adjusting these when you start the network. Using the NET command and the menu option permits you to alter six of these parameters on startup. Using the NET SHARE command permits you to alter all of them. For more details, see Chapter 12, 13, 17 and Appendix B.

You may decide at any time to change the session name, the configuration, or the startup parameters. The easiest way to do this is to edit the AUTOEXEC.BAT file, changing the desired values. Use any word processor in the non-document mode, or an editor. You must then reboot the system to start the network using the new AUTOEXEC.BAT file. If the system is a server you should be sure no user is using it before rebooting. Broadcast message to all users, then display the status and be sure no users are using the server.

Another way to reconfigure the network is to boot the system without starting the network (by answering N to the prompt), then using the NET command and menus, or the NET START command, to reconfigure the network, saving it as a new configuration file.

Chapter 12

Starting
the Server:
Sharing Resources

T HE NEXT STEP IN GETTING THE NETWORK OPERATIONAL IS TO ALLO-
cate resources. You can install the systems in any order. You can even
start the network on the systems in any order. The next step, however, *must*
be initiated on the server before a user can use the shared resource.

Using resources across the network involves two phases: the resource that
is to be shared must be offered by the server, and the user must request to
use it on a workstation. This is similar to any type of resource sharing. If you
have a tractor lawnmower and a neighbor wishes to use it, there are the same
two steps. First, you must offer to share the mower. Second, the neighbor must
accept your offer to share the mower.

A server is the only configuration that can make an offer to share a resource. The offer to share can be made in any one of three ways: from the
network main menu, with the NET SHARE command, or from the
AUTOEXEC.BAT file on startup. This chapter shows you how to use all three
methods.

The offer to share assigns a network name to a directory or printer. For
example, we could use the NET SHARE command to assign the name PUBLIC
to the C:\APPS public directory on the server. After this, anyone on the
network could request to use this directory using the PUBLIC name.

Once you have offered to share a resource, any workstation (regardless
of its configuration) can request use of a shared resource. When a workstation
requests use of a resource, it assigns a disk drive designator to the network
name. For example, a workstation could assign \\SERVER1\PUBLIC to

a disk drive K (see Fig. 12-1). After this the user does not need to use the longer network name to refer to files on the public directory again, but can simply use the drive designator.

This makes it unnecessary to modify any programs on the workstation or make other operational changes. The subdirectory on the server has become a *virtual* disk drive on the workstation. When a workstation program makes a request to read or write using the virtual disk drive, the *PC LAN* software traps the request and redirects it to the network name. The server, in turn, traps the request using the network name and redirects it to the proper subdirectory. This is the basic function of the redirector "shell" that is a part of the *PC LAN* on both the server and workstation. The user's private directory on the server becomes a virtual disk drive on the workstation.

Once you have offered to share resources on a server, you should again save your configuration in the AUTOEXEC.BAT file. This will save your current offers to share in the file as NET SHARE commands, and the next time you boot your system the network will start again with the same resources shared.

SHARING DIRECTORY RESOURCES

If you are starting the computers in your network for the first time, be sure both systems in the test configuration are started on *PC LAN* before continuing (Chapter 11).

Once you have started the network on each computer, a user at a workstation now has access to the network, but still cannot use any directories on the server or use the server printer. The server must offer to make these resources available before a workstation can use them. Your next job should be to offer the resources on the server that will be shared.

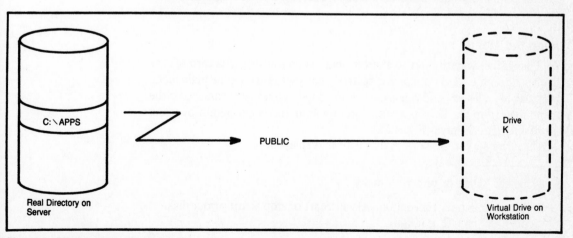

C:\APPS

PUBLIC

Drive K

Real Directory on Server

Virtual Drive on Workstation

Fig. 12-1. Offering to share a resource.

The server's offer to share resources is a general offer to the network. The server does not offer a directory or printer to a specific machine or user, but each offer is always made to all workstations on the network. Even the private directories are offered to everyone. The names of the private directories, however, are only disclosed to the individual users.

There is one exception to this—the use of the PERMIT command (this will be discussed later). If the user knows the session name of the server (for example, SERVER1) and the name of the resource (such as PUBLIC), any workstation can use the resource once it has been offered.

Once you have offered to share a resource, the offer is not published on the network (or made known to other users). The server name, as well as the network name of the resource and the fact that it is available, cannot be obtained using a workstation from the network itself. Network resource names can be secured, if desired, with passwords. The server operator or administrator must maintain records of what is available and distribute this information to users. In a secured environment, you may wish to change network names and passwords daily, weekly, or monthly.

As when starting the network, you can define the resources on the server you plan to share in any of three ways: using the main menu, using the NET SHARE command with parameters, or by using an AUTOEXEC.BAT file.

Each resource must be shared using a separate command or menu call. For example, suppose the server contained one printer to be shared, one public APPS directory, and two private user directories. This would require the use of four commands.

Note: You can share a hard disk directory or a printer, but you should avoid sharing a floppy disk directory. The *PC Local Area Network* software will permit this, but if two users try to use the same disk you can lose data. Use this strategy only for temporary support of an auxiliary disk drive by a single user.

Using the Menu

The easiest way to offer to share resources on the server is through the main menu. If the DOS prompt is displayed, you always access the main menu by typing NET < Return >. If you are a server or messenger, you can access the main menu from the DOS prompt or from within another program by using the Ctrl/Alt/Break keys (Fig. 12-2).

Once the server network main menu is displayed:

1. Select "Disk or directory tasks."

2. On the menu for this option, select "Start or stop sharing your disk or directory" (Fig. 12-3).

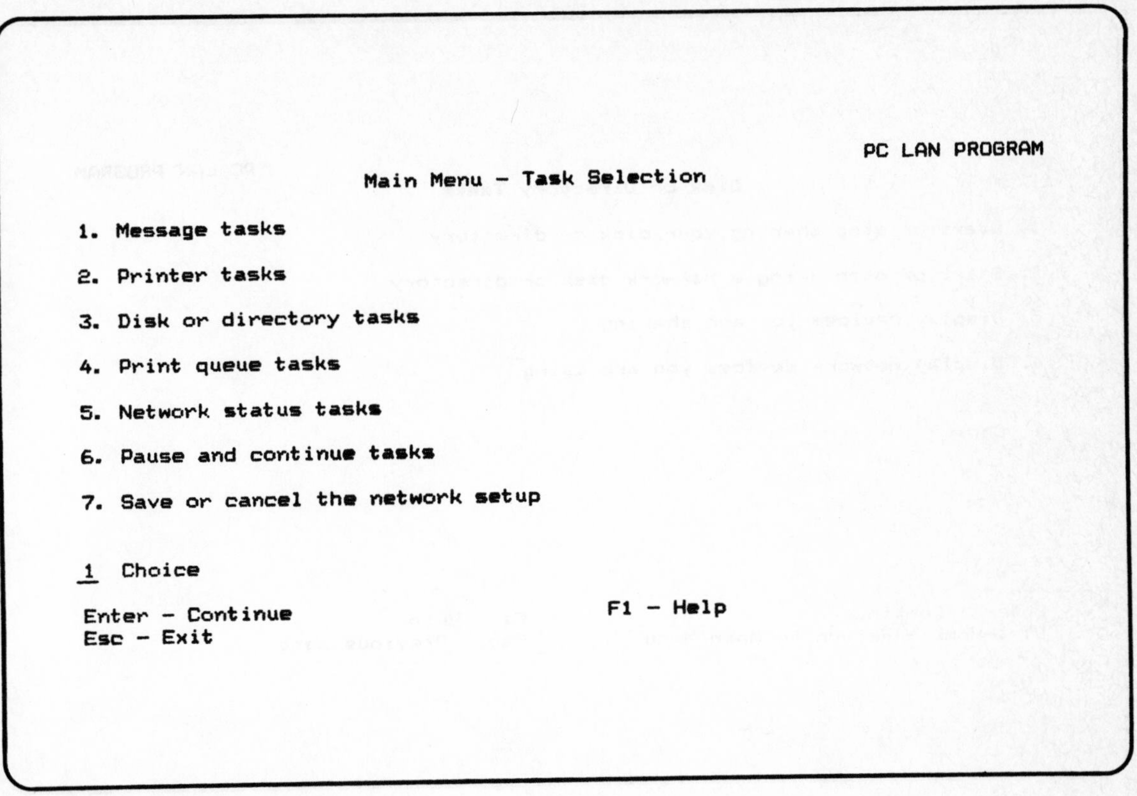

```
                                                    PC LAN PROGRAM
                Main Menu — Task Selection

   1.  Message tasks

   2.  Printer tasks

   3.  Disk or directory tasks

   4.  Print queue tasks

   5.  Network status tasks

   6.  Pause and continue tasks

   7.  Save or cancel the network setup


   1  Choice

   Enter — Continue                    F1 — Help
   Esc — Exit
```

Fig. 12-2. The server main menu.

3. On the next menu, select "Start sharing your disk or directory" (Fig. 12-4).

4. A form is now displayed (Fig. 12-5) that must be filled in. Use the Tab key to move between options on the form. Use the following guidelines to complete the form:

   a) Enter the name of the directory you wish to share, such as C:\APPS.

   b) Enter the network name by which users will access this directory, such as PUBLIC.

   c) If you wish to use a password, enter the password. This is optional.

   d) Pick an access level. This controls what users can do with files in the directory. Whatever you select here will apply to all files

```
                                                        PC LAN PROGRAM
                    Disk or Directory Tasks

    1. Start or stop sharing your disk or directory

    2. Start or stop using a network disk or directory

    3. Display devices you are sharing

    4. Display network devices you are using


    1  Choice




    Enter - Continue                    F1 - Help
    Ctrl-Home - Return to Main Menu      Esc - Previous menu
```

Fig. 12-3. Selecting the disk or directory task.

in the directory. Option 5 (Read/Write/Create/Delete) is the default option, unless it is changed. If you need to control access to specific files in the directory, use the DOS ATTRIB command external to *PC Network*, but note that if a file attribute is set to read-only with the ATTRIB command or by the Installation Aid, you will not be able to override that here.

e) Document the entry for your records in a notebook before pressing the Enter key.

f) Once you have completed and documented your entries, press <Enter>. You will see a message that the directory is now shared, and the form (now blank) will be displayed again.

g) Continue to enter each directory you wish to share. Once all directory resources have been defined, press <Esc> to exit to the main menu.

Pressing the Enter key indicates you have completed the form entry.

You may offer the same resource (directory) with different access codes for different users by offering it two or more times with different network names and the appropriate access code.

Using the NET SHARE Command

You can bypass the menus and share a resource using a direct command with the NET SHARE command. The proper command form is:

NET SHARE *network_name = path password /access*

where:

network_name	=	the name by which the resource will be identified by the users.
path	=	the path or directory on the server that is being shared.

```
                                                      PC LAN PROGRAM
         Start or Stop Sharing Your Disk or Directory

 1. Start sharing your disk or directory

 2. Stop sharing your disk or directory


 1  Choice




 Enter - Continue                    F1 - Help
 Ctrl-Home - Return to Main Menu      Esc - Previous menu
```

Fig. 12-4. Starting the sharing of a directory.

```
                                                       PC LAN PROGRAM
                Start Sharing Your Disk or Directory

DOS name for disk or directory
     C:\APPS

Network name for your disk or directory
     PUBLIC

Password for disk or directory (Optional)
     _____

Other users can
1. Read only              4. Write/Create/Delete
2. Read/Write             5. Read/Write/Create/Delete
3. Write only

5  Choice
__

     Tab - Cursor to next field
     Enter - Continue
     Esc - Previous menu              F1 - Help
                                      Ctrl-Home - Return to Main Menu
```

Fig. 12-5. The form for sharing a directory.

password	=	optional password for this session.
access	=	the access code (r = read, w = write, c = create and delete)

For example, to open the public directory as PUBLIC for any type of access and no password use:

NET SHARE PUBLIC = C: \ APPS /RWC

It is possible to share a resource using the NET SHARE command without specifying a network name. If the network name is omitted, users must reference the resource using the full path name on the server. Omitting the network name is normally a poor practice and should be avoided, as it exposes the users to the true directory structure and also makes it more difficult to withdraw the offer to share.

Automatic Sharing

When a configuration with shared resources is saved in the AUTOEXEC.BAT file, the configuration for the currently shared resources is saved as NET SHARE commands in the AUTOEXEC.BAT file. When the computer is subsequently booted and the network started, the same resources are shared again with the same network names and access. Passwords are not saved, and must be reentered again on restarting. Do not save your configuration at this time, as you have not yet completed your resource allocation.

PRINTER ALLOCATION

As with directories, a server must specifically offer to the network any printer that will be shared by other workstations. As with offering a directory, you can use the menu, the NET SHARE command, or the AUTOEXEC.BAT file.

Using the Menu

You can display the main menu from the DOS prompt by using the NET command. You can display it from the prompt or any application program by using the Ctrl/Alt/Break keys.

1. On the main menu, select "Printer tasks."

2. On the next option menu (Fig. 12-6), select "Start or stop sharing your printer."

3. On the next option screen (Fig. 12-7), select "Start sharing your printer."

4. Fill in the form that is displayed (Fig. 12-8):

   a) Enter the DOS name for the printer (LPT1, LPT2, etc.).

   b) Enter the network name you have assigned to the printer (such as LASER).

   c) Enter a password, if desired. The password is optional.

5. When the form entry is completed, press <Enter>.

Using the Command Line

You can also offer to share a printer using the NET SHARE command. The general form for this command is:

NET SHARE *network__name = DOSname*

```
                                                        PC LAN PROGRAM
                     Printer Tasks

    1. Start or stop sharing your printer

    2. Start or stop using a network printer

    3. Print a file

    4. Change the print size on a network printer

    5. Display devices you are sharing

    6. Display network devices you are using


    1  Choice



    Enter - Continue                    F1 - Help
    Ctrl-Home - Return to Main Menu     Esc - Previous menu
```

Fig. 12-6. Selecting the printer task.

For example:

    C> NET SHARE LASER = LPT1   <Enter>

Automating Printer Sharing

You can save your configuration at any time and the NET SHARE commands that allocate the current sharing of resources will be saved as part of the AUTOEXEC.BAT file. The next time you boot your system and request to start the network, the printer will automatically be shared.

Special Notes on Printer Sharing—When you make an offer to share a printer on the network, *PC LAN* automatically makes a second offer, using as a network name the DOS name with an underline prefix. For example, if you offered to share LPT1 as LASER, it will also be offered as __LPT1. At the same time, any requests to print on the server that would normally go to LPT1 are redirected to __LPT1. The net effect of this is that printer output from the server is directed to the same print queue used by all systems on the network.

USING PASSWORDS

If a password is used when a resource is offered, the password applies only to the current session. The password is not saved in an AUTOEXEC.BAT file for future network startups. (This is what you would want to happen; otherwise someone could find the passwords by examining the AUTOEXEC.BAT file.) The AUTOEXEC.BAT file only shows asterisks in the NET SHARE command line where the password would normally be entered. The next time you start the network from the AUTOEXEC.BAT file and the offer is made from this file to share the same resource using a NET SHARE command, *PC LAN* only remembers that you used a password. You will be prompted for a new password.

If you wish, you can edit the AUTOEXEC.BAT file, replacing the asterisks

```
                                                      PC LAN PROGRAM
              Start or Stop Sharing Your Printer

  1. Start sharing your printer

  2. Stop sharing your printer


  1  Choice









  Enter - Continue                      F1 - Help
  Ctrl-Home - Return to Main Menu       Esc - Previous menu
```

Fig. 12-7. Starting to share a printer.

```
                                                        PC LAN PROGRAM
                      Start Sharing Your Printer

   DOS name for printer
       LPT1      (LPT1, LPT2, ...)

   Network name for your printer
       LASER

   Password for printer (Optional)
       ───────




       Tab - Cursor to next field
       Enter - Continue             F1 - Help
       Esc - Previous menu          Ctrl-Home - Return to Main Menu
```

Fig. 12-8. Filling in the form to share a printer.

with passwords. The system will boot correctly, using the passwords in the file. Anyone who examines the AUTOEXEC.BAT file, however, could then discover the passwords.

You can secure your network without passwords simply by using secret network names for resources that you do not wish to make public (such as FGRTZ). In most cases this would be sufficient security. To prevent unauthorized access to directories, you would need to secure access to the server from unauthorized personnel. Either network names or passwords could be changed daily if necessary.

WITHDRAWING OFFERS TO SHARE

Once you have made an offer to share a resource, you can also withdraw the offer so the resource is no longer available. To withdraw an offer using the menu:

1. Display the main menu using NET or the Ctrl/Alt/Break keys.

2. Select "Disk or directory tasks" or "Printer tasks."

3. On the next option, select "Start or stop sharing your disk or directory" or "Start or stop sharing your printer."

4. On the next screen, select "Stop sharing the printer."

5. Enter the network name of the directory or printer to withdraw (Fig. 12-9) and press <Enter>.

The offer is then withdrawn, and you will see a confirmation message. You can also use the NET SHARE command to withdraw an offer. Use the command name with the network name and a /D, as in:

C> NET SHARE LASER /D <Enter>

With the NET SHARE command it is not necessary to specify a network when an offer is made to share a resource. In doing this, however, it makes it more difficult to withdraw the offer. If no network name was specified, you

```
                                                              PC LAN PROGRAM
              Start or Stop Sharing Your Disk or Directory

     1. Start sharing your disk or directory

     2. Stop sharing your disk or directory


        2  Choice

Network name for your disk or directory
        PUBLIC




        Tab - Cursor to next field
        Enter - Continue                  F1 - Help
        Esc - Previous menu                Ctrl-Home - Return to Main Menu
```

Fig. 12-9. Withdrawing an offer to share.

must specify the access code when withdrawing the offer. The resource may have been shared more than once with different access codes, and this is the only way the computer would know which offer to withdraw.

Withdrawing an offer to share can cause problems for users on the network who are using that resource. Check with network users before withdrawing any resource that may be in use. Broadcast a message, then use the network program to display the current network users, so you can be sure no one is using the resource. Withdrawing an offer to share while print jobs are still in the queue, and then doing a screen dump on the printer, can create serious network problems.

USING STARTUP PARAMETERS

You can use the SHR parameter when starting *PC LAN* to define the maximum number of directories and printers that can be shared by the server. The default number is 10. If you do not alter the parameter, you can have a maximum of 10 NET SHARE statements in the AUTOEXEC.BAT file. The parameter is used to build a table; the table requires 350 bytes for each resource permitted. The maximum value is 150.

If you wish to change the SHR value, you must restart the network. You can change it from the start menu by rejecting the defaults. You can also change it with the NET START command by adding the appropriate parameter:

```
C> NET START SRV SERVER1 /SHR:25 <Enter>
```

You should also save the new configuration so the value will be used the next time you start the network.

Another alternative for changing the SHR value is to edit the AUTOEXEC.BAT file and then restart the network.

DOCUMENTING YOUR WORK

You should document your configuration on the server and then save the installation. There is no option for printing a report using *PC LAN*. You must display the status and then do a screen dump.

To display a status from the menu, select either "Printer Tasks" or "Disk or directory tasks" (both display the same status report). On the next option menu, select "Display devices you are sharing." A status report will be displayed (Fig. 12-10). From the command mode, you can obtain this same report by entering NET SHARE with no arguments. Dump the screen using Shift/PrtSc.

If you have shared a printer, you will not be able to dump the report using

```
                                                          PC LAN PROGRAM
                        Display Devices You Are Sharing

Access/     Network        DOS
Status      Name           Name                   Names Using the Device
─────────────────────────────────────────────────────────────────────────
                           LPT1
SYSTEM      _LPT1          LPT1                    SERVER1
   RWC      PUBLIC         C:\APPS
                           -- End of share list --


─────────────────────────────────────────────────────────────────────────
      PgUp and PgDn - Scroll list
      Enter - Redisplay list                F1 - Help
      Ctrl-Home - Return to Main Menu        Esc - Previous menu
```

Fig. 12-10. Displaying the status.

Shift/PrtSc. To dump the report you must temporarily suspend the use of the printer on the network using NET PAUSE PRDR from the C> prompt. You can also issue the command from within a *PC LAN* display (such as the status display) using the <F2> key. To restore printer sharing, use NET CONTINUE PRDR.

The report shows the DOS name or path for each entry, the network name, the access status and the names of all current users. The names listed under "Names Using the Device" represent the session names of anyone who has issued a NET USE command on the device or directory. It does not necessarily mean that any file is open on the directory, or that the printer is printing. For more specific file information, you must use the NET FILE command.

SAVING CONFIGURATIONS

Before starting and configuring the workstations, you should save the current configuration of the server. From the main menu, select "Save or cancel the network setup." On the next option menu, select "Save your network setup."

Chapter 13

Using Resources:
The Workstation

O NCE YOU HAVE STARTED ALL THE SERVERS IN THE NETWORK, YOU should start each workstation in the network. If you are using the two-computer test configuration mentioned in Chapter 10, you should leave the server in this configuration and connect each workstation in turn (one at a time) to start each. Chapter 11 described the process of starting the workstation.

You cannot use a resource unless it has been offered by a server. Be sure you have started the servers in your configuration and offered the resources you wish to share before continuing with this chapter.

Two types of resources on the server can be made available for a workstation to use: directory resources and printer resources.

DIRECTORY RESOURCES

When you make a request from a workstation to use a server directory resource, you assign a local disk drive designator to a server directory. The directory name is identified on the network by the server session name and the network name of the directory on the server. After the assignment is made you can use the directory just as you would use a directory on a local disk (Fig. 13-1). The disk drive designator used must be equal to or less than the designator specified by LASTDRIVE in the CONFIG.SYS file. If not specified in the CONFIG.SYS file, the last drive becomes N.

On the server, for example, you could assign the C:\APPS subdirectory to PUBLIC. On the workstation you could assign the PUBLIC directory on

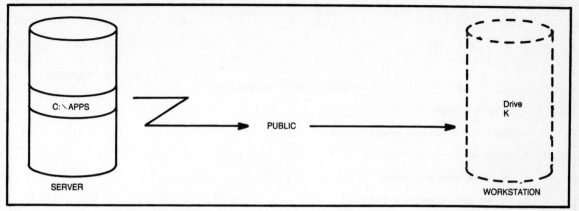

Fig. 13-1. Taking up an offer and using a resource.

SERVER1 to disk drive K. Once this is done, you could switch to Drive K on the workstation and execute a program on the server's C:\APPS subdirectory. Disk drive K is said to be a *virtual* (not real, but functioning as if it were) disk drive on the local computer, and the workstation could use it just as if it were a hard disk on the workstation.

You can also modify the PATH command on the workstation so that when a request is made to execute a program, the workstation searches both the current directory on the local computer and the public directory on the server.

Now let us see how to request use of a directory resource. There are three ways you can ask to use a server's directory resources from a workstation: use the *PC LAN* main menu, use the NET USE command, or use an AUTOEXEC.BAT file.

Using the Menu

The menu alternative is the easiest. The main menu is reached using the NET command, or the Ctrl/Alt/Break keys at the DOS prompt, or by using Ctrl/Alt/Break from within an active program. Notice that the workstation menu (Fig. 13-2) is slightly different from the server menu (Fig. 11-5). Once the main menu is displayed:

1. Select "Disk or directory tasks."

2. On the next option menu (Fig. 13-3), select "Start or stop using a network disk or directory."

3. On the next option menu (Fig. 13-4), select "Start using a network disk or directory."

4. You will then see a form (Fig. 13-5) that you can use to fill in the details. Use the Tab key to move between items on the form. Use

```
                                                      PC LAN PROGRAM
                    Main Menu - Task Selection

    1. Message tasks

    2. Printer or print queue tasks

    3. Disk or directory tasks

    4. Network status tasks

    5. Pause and continue tasks

    6. Save or cancel the network setup


    3  Choice
    ‾

    Enter - Continue                      F1 - Help
    Esc - Exit
```

Fig. 13-2. The workstation main menu.

the Enter key to indicate you have completed the form entry.

a) Enter the name of the computer on which the disk or directory
   is located (for example, SERVER1).

b) Enter the network name of the directory (for example, PUBLIC).

c) Enter the DOS drive you wish this assigned to on your
   workstation computer.

d) Enter a password. (This is optional).

Press the Enter key to complete the assignment. The computer will
acknowledge the assignment with a message, then display a blank form.
Continue with additional assignments as you wish. When you have made all
the requests necessary, press <Esc> to terminate the process.

The NET USE Command

From the command prompt, you can use the NET USE command to

request the use of a resource on the server. The general form of the command is:

NET USE *drive* \ \ *server__name* \ *network__name password*

where:

drive	=	drive designator
server__name	=	session name of server offering the resource
network__name	=	network name of resource
password	=	optional password

When using the command form, the use of the disk drive specification is optional. If omitted, the user must use the path name (server and network name) to access a file on the directory. It is a good practice, however, to always specify a drive.

Automatic Use Requests

As on the server, you can save your current workstation configuration as

```
                                                        PC LAN PROGRAM
                    Disk or Directory Tasks

1. Start or stop using a network disk or directory

2. Display network devices you are using


1  Choice






Enter - Continue                     F1 - Help
Ctrl-Home - Return to Main Menu      Esc - Previous menu
```

Fig. 13-3. Selecting the disk or directory task.

```
                                                        PC LAN PROGRAM
          Start or Stop Using a Network Disk or Directory

  1. Start using a network disk or directory

  2. Stop using a network disk or directory


  1  Choice
  _




  Enter - Continue                    F1 - Help
  Ctrl-Home - Return to Main Menu     Esc - Previous menu
```

Fig. 13-4. Starting to use a directory.

a series of commands in an AUTOEXEC.BAT file. The current session name, configuration, parameters, and resource requests will all be saved as NET START and NET USE commands. You can then make automatic requests to use resources each time the system is booted and the network is started.

PRINTER RESOURCES

Before you can use a printer on the server you must request its use. As with directory resources, you can use any of three methods to request the use of printer resources: the menu alternative, the NET USE command, and automatic requests.

Using the Menu

The menu alternative is the easiest method of requesting to use a printer. The main menu is obtained on a workstation using the NET command, or the

Ctrl/Alt/Break keys at the DOS prompt, or by using Ctrl/Alt/Break from within an active program. Once the main menu is displayed:

1. Select "Printer tasks."

2. On the next option menu (Fig. 13-6), select "Start or stop using a network printer."

3. On the next option menu (Fig. 13-7), select "Start using a network printer."

4. You will then see a form (Fig. 13-8) that you can use to fill in the details. Use the Tab key to move between items on the form. Use the Enter key to indicate you have completed the form entry. Enter the session name of the server, the network name of the printer, and the DOS name you wish to use for the printer on your own local computer. You can also enter an optional password.

```
                                                          PC LAN PROGRAM
                    Start Using a Network Disk or Directory

Disk or Directory is on computer
      SERVER1

Network name of disk or directory
      PUBLIC

DOS drive name on your computer for network disk or directory
      K (A, B, C, ...)

Password for disk or directory (Optional)
      _____




      Tab - Cursor to next field
      Enter - Continue                  F1 - Help
      Esc - Previous menu               Ctrl-Home - Return to Main Menu
```

Fig. 13-5. The form for using a directory.

```
                                                              PC LAN PROGRAM
                      Printer and Print Queue Tasks

        1. Check print queue on another computer

        2. Start or stop using a network printer

        3. Print a file

        4. Change the print size on a network printer

        5. Display network devices you are using


        2  Choice




        Enter - Continue                      F1 - Help
        Ctrl-Home - Return to Main Menu       Esc - Previous menu
```

Fig. 13-6. Selecting a printer task.

5. Press <Enter> to complete the assignment. You will see a confirmation message, after which a blank form will be displayed to assign another printer.

6. When all printers have been requested, press <Esc> to exit.

Using the Command Form

You can also use the NET USE command to request use of a printer. The general form of the command is:

NET USE *DOSname* \ \ *server_name* \ *network_name password*

As an example:

NET USE LPT1: \ \ SERVER1 \ LASER

126

Using the Automatic Form

As with directory requests, you can save the current configuration in the AUTOEXEC.BAT file. Once saved, the workstation can be automatically configured (with the use of the network printer requested) on booting.

Special Notes on Using the Printer—When a server offers to share a printer under a network name, it is also offered under the corresponding DOS name, preceded by an underline. For example, if a laser printer is offered as LASER and redirected to LPT1, a second offer is made automatically. The laser printer will also be offered under __LPT1.

At the user end, you might request to use it as LASER, assigning it to LPT2. The workstation also automatically makes a second user request, requesting to use __LPT1 as LPT1. The result is that any print output directed to LPT1 on the workstation printer will be directed to the laser printer on the server, even though the user never requested this assignment.

```
                                                      PC LAN PROGRAM
            Start or Stop Using a Network Printer

  1. Start using a network printer

  2. Stop using a network printer


  1  Choice
  ‾









  Enter - Continue                    F1 - Help
  Ctrl-Home - Return to Main Menu     Esc - Previous menu
```

Fig. 13-7. Selecting to use a network printer.

```
                                                        PC LAN PROGRAM
                    Start Using a Network Printer

    Printer is on computer
        SERVER

    Network name of printer
        LASER

    DOS name on your computer for network printer
        LPT1 (LPT1, LPT2, LPT3)

    Password for printer (Optional)
        _____



        Tab - Cursor to next field
        Enter - Continue               F1 - Help
        Esc - Previous menu            Ctrl-Home - Return to Main Menu
```

Fig. 13-8. The form to use a network printer.

You can use the DOS MODE command to redirect printer output as well as control special features of printing, such as the number of characters per line.

WITHDRAWING OFFERS TO USE

You can withdraw an offer to use a printer or directory at any time. You can use the main menu or the NET USE command to withdraw offers.

Using the Main Menu

To withdraw an offer using the main menu, display the menu using the NET command or the Ctrl/Alt/Break keys.

1. Select "Disk or directory tasks" or "Printer tasks."

2. On the next option screen, select "Start or stop sharing your disk or directory" or "Start or stop sharing your printer."

3. On the next menu, select the stop option.

4. Fill in the form (Fig. 13-9), supplying the network name of the directory or printer.

5. An acknowledgment message will be displayed. Press <Esc> to exit the form.

Withdrawing with NET USE

You can also withdraw the use of a resource by using the NET USE command with a /D parameter. Include the device name (such as LPT1) or drive name (such as K). Include nothing more, and do not use the password. For example:

C > USE LPT1 \ D   <Enter>

STARTUP PARAMETERS THAT CONTROL SHARING

When the system is started from the menu (using NET) or using NET START you can specify parameters that control the space allocated for tables

```
                                                          PC LAN PROGRAM
         Start or Stop Using a Network Disk or Directory

   1. Start using a network disk or directory

   2. Stop using a network disk or directory


      2  Choice

DOS drive name on your computer for network disk or directory
      K (A, B, C, ...)




   Tab - Cursor to next field
   Enter - Continue                    F1 - Help
   Esc - Previous menu                 Ctrl-Home - Return to Main Menu
```

Fig. 13-9. Withdrawing an offer to use a directory.

that save the information on resources that are in use. The two parameters that affect using resources are SRV and ASG:

SRV: Maximum number of servers in the network. This defaults to 2, but can be set as high as 31.

ASG: Maximum number of network directories and printers in use. Defines the number of NET USE commands that can be active at one time. This defaults to 5, but can be set as high as 32.

ASG can be set from the main startup menu. SRV can only be set using the NET START command.

SAVING AND PRINTING THE CONFIGURATION

After you have made all the requests for all the resources you will use, save the configuration. From the main menu, select "Save or cancel the network setup." Select "Save your network setup" on the next menu. An acknowledgment message will be displayed.

You should also display a copy of the allocations for verification. This can be done from the main menu or by using a command. *PC LAN* will only permit you to display the report. You cannot print the report. If a printer is shared, you cannot dump the screen using Shift/PrtSc.

To display the report from the main menu, select "Printer tasks" or "Disk or directory tasks." On the next menu, select "Display devices you are using." The report shows all the allocations you have made with the NET USE command. If the workstation does not share or use a printer, you can print the report by dumping the screen on any local printer using Shift/PrtSc.

You can display the same report from the DOS prompt using NET USE with no parameters.

Chapter 14

Sending and Receiving Messages

THE *PC LAN* SOFTWARE INCLUDES A SIMPLE MESSAGE SYSTEM THAT CAN be used to send, edit, and receive messages. This chapter will introduce you to the basic concepts of using this system.

THE MESSAGE SYSTEM

The *PC Local Area Network* message system is a very important feature that can be used in many creative ways. Remember that the network does not publish information about itself. Network resource names and resource names are not available to the user with any network or DOS command. As a result, it is up to the network users to maintain a level of communication about what resources are available and the status of the network. This is where the message system becomes important. A server operator would normally broadcast a message on the network notifying users about network names that can be used and the status of printers and other features. The message system can also be used to define conventions and procedures.

The *PC LAN* message system is not meant to serve as an elaborate electronic mail system. There is no storage facility at the sending end for the message if the receiver is not available. Once a message is composed, it is sent immediately. You cannot save a message as a file and send it again at a later time. Messages must either be sent to a single individual or to everyone on the network: you cannot send a message to a group of people. Messages are always short, with the length limited to 11 lines or less when using the menu mode and a single line when using the command mode.

The messaging capabilities of a system on the network are limited by the configuration of the system. A server has the use of all the messaging features. A redirector, in contrast, has the use of the fewest features.

Any system in the network can *send* a message regardless of its configuration. In any configuration, you can send a message at any time using either the menu mode or command mode.

Receiving is another story. Only the server, messenger, and receiver configurations can receive messages. If you try to send a message to a system in a redirector configuration, you will get an error message. The redirector can only send messages or use directories and printers.

There are three ways to receive a message: using a log file, using a buff-er, or immediate. Only the messenger and server configurations can use all three methods. The receiver configuration can only use two of these. Let us look for a moment at each method of receiving messages.

The Log File

This method directs incoming messages to a separate log file, where they are read at the user's convenience. To use this method requires nothing more than the user defining a log file where incoming messages will be stored. Once this is done, any incoming message is directed to and saved in the log file. The user hears four beeps, indicating a message has been saved. Except for the beeps, the user is not disturbed. Later, when the user is not busy, the log file can be scanned and the message retrieved.

This method can be used by server, messenger, or receiver configurations. (The redirector cannot receive messages.) The log file is most advantageous if the user is working on a project requiring a high level of concentration and does not wish to be disturbed. The disadvantage is that the user does not see the message immediately, hearing only the beeps. The receiving system cannot respond immediately to any questions in the message.

Using the Buffer

With buffered reception, incoming messages force a display of a simple indicator, "Message from XXXX" in a small box in the center of the screen (with the name of the sending computer). The message overlays any current screen contents.

If the user wishes to view the message immediately, it is only necessary to press the Ctrl/Alt/Break keys. If he does not wish to view the message immediately, pressing the Ctrl/Break keys will direct the message to a buffer where it can be read later. To reply to the message, the F4 key switches to a separate Send screen to enter a reply. Once the viewing (or viewing and sending) is completed, the screen is restored to the former display. The F3 key can be used at any time to view the oldest message in the buffer and delete it.

In this mode, the F4 key acts as a toggle, switching between the View screen with the incoming message and the Send screen which can be used to compose an outgoing message. In this way the user can view the incoming message again at any time while editing a reply.

This method is available for the server and messenger configurations, and is perhaps the most flexible approach for most users.

Immediate Viewing

If you are using the receiver configuration and have not defined a log file, there is no buffer. Messages are displayed immediately on receipt. There is no message buffer and no view screen. The message will overlay any current screen contents, and the screen will not be restored after the message is displayed. This approach is the least desirable in most applications. If you are using the receiver configuration, you will probably always want to define a log file for messages. This is the default mode in the receiver configuration, so it is best in this configuration to always define a log file.

SENDING MESSAGES

Messages can be sent using either the command mode or the menu mode. Let us look at both methods.

The Command Mode

Using the NET SEND command, you can send a short message to any individual on the network or to everyone on the network. The general form of the command is:

C > NET SEND *destination_name message*

where:

> *destination_name* = session name of destination system.
> *message* = message

You are limited to a total line length of whatever your DOS will support, normally about 130 characters. For example, to send a message to JANE telling her that the printer is ready, you could enter:

C > NET SEND JANE The printer is ready now. < Enter >

You may use upper- or lowercase letters, and the letters will be transmitted in the same case as you enter them. Once you have pressed the carriage re-

133

turn or Enter key, you will see a message acknowledging the fact that the message was successfully received. The message is somewhat misleading, because the transmitting station has no way to determine whether the message is received or not.

If you wish to broadcast a message to everyone on the network, use the asterisk as the destination name.

C > NET SEND * The printer is ready < Enter >

If you need to send a message longer than the command mode will support, use the menu mode.

The Menu Mode

The menu mode permits you to send messages up to 1600 characters or 11 lines, whichever is less (you can, of course, elect to use very long lines). You also have available a small editor when composing your message.

The Send Screen. To send messages using the menu mode of *PC LAN*, use the Send screen of the message module. The message module in *PC LAN* supports two screens. One is a Send screen, the second a View screen. The Send screen is used to compose and edit messages before sending. The View screen is used to view received messages. You can switch rapidly between the two screens using the function keys, making it possible to view any incoming message and quickly compose a reply, viewing the received message again as necessary.

To send a message, there are two ways to access the edit screen:

1. You can use the NET command from the DOS prompt or Ctrl/Alt/Break from any program or the DOS prompt. Select "Message Tasks" from the main menu. On the next menu select "Send messages" (Fig. 14-1).
2. If you are receiving a message and wish to reply, you can use the F4 key while viewing the message to exit the View screen to the Send screen.

Once the Send screen is displayed (Fig. 14-2), you can enter the destination name, after which you should tab to the message area and enter the message. You may send the message to any valid session name on the network (except those with a redirector configuration). You can use the asterisk to indicate a destination name if the message should be sent to all users.

You have 11 lines which can be used to enter a message, for a maximum of 1600 characters. As you enter the message, an automatic word-wrap is in effect—if a word you enter extends beyond the right margin, a carriage return will be entered and the entire word will move to the next line. The word-wrap

```
                                                    PC LAN PROGRAM
              Message Tasks

1. Send messages

2. View received messages

3. Start or stop saving messages

4. Start or stop receiving messages for another name

5. Start or stop forwarding messages

6. Display names that can receive messages at your computer


1  Choice



Enter - Continue                      F1 - Help
Ctrl-Home - Return to Main Menu       Esc - Previous menu
```

Fig.14-1. Starting a message task.

does not work, however, if you are editing and inserting or deleting text. After you edit the text you can, however, force a reformat by pressing the F3 key. This reformats the entire paragraph from the current cursor position.

The editing capability for message entry is very limited, but a few commands are available. The Del key deletes the character under the current cursor position. The Ins key acts as a toggle to switch you to the insert mode. In the insert mode, as you enter new characters at the cursor position, characters to the right of the cursor are pushed to the right. In the normal mode, any text entered will overwrite existing text. The Home key will take you to the beginning of the current line, and the End key will take you to the end of the line.

Unlike other menu screens, the Enter key is not used to exit the screen. While entering the message, the Enter key is used to terminate each line of the message.

Sending the Message. Once you have completed the message entry, you can send the message using Ctrl/Enter. You will then see an acknowledgment message near the end of the screen. The destination address and message remain on the screen, so you can edit either the destination address or message and send another message. You can clear the entire message area using Ctrl/PgDn to enter another message.

To leave the editor screen, use either Esc or Ctrl/Home. Esc returns you to where you entered the screen, and Ctrl/Home returns you to the network main menu.

RECEIVING MESSAGES

A receiver can use a log file or immediate viewing. The default mode (no log file specified) is immediate viewing. A server or messenger can use a log file, buffered viewing, or immediate viewing.

Using a Log File

In the server, messenger, or receiver configurations you can elect to save incoming messages in a log file. To initiate this mode, it is only necessary to

```
                              Send Messages                    PC LAN PROGRAM

Send the message to: (* for all computers)  __*_____

Type message below :
_____
The printer is ready.




_____
Ctrl-Enter - Send message          Esc - Previous menu or Exit
Tab - Cursor to next field         Ctrl-PgDn - Erase message
F1 HELP/MORE KEYS    F2 COMMAND LINE    F3 ADJUST PARAGRAPH F4 VIEW MESSAGES
F5 RETRIEVE FIRST    F6 RETRIEVE NEXT   F7 SAVE MESSAGE

                                            Characters Free   106
```

Fig. 14-2. Sending a message.

define the log file. You may use the menu mode or command mode to define this file.

To use the command mode to define a log file, use the NET LOG command as:

C > NET LOG *filename* < Enter >

Be sure to specify the log file extension name (LOG). Avoid using a log file on the server when saving messages on a workstation. It will work, but it is a bad practice.

As an example, to save messages in a log file MSG.LOG on Drive B, use:

C > NET LOG B: \ MSG.LOG < Enter >

If the file does not exist, it will be created. Incoming messages are always appended to the current messages in the active log file. You can, if you wish, specify the printer as the output device by using PRN as the file name. Be careful, however, that you do not direct the printer output to the server. It will still work, but you will generally wish to direct the log output to a local device—either a file or printer.

To terminate the use of the log file, use the / off parameter without a file name:

C > NET LOG /off < Enter >

You can resume the use of the current log file with the /on parameter:

C > NET LOG /on < Enter >

You can also resume with another log file by using the NET LOG command with another file name.

You can also use the network main menu to initiate or terminate the use of a log file. Activate the main menu using the NET command or Ctrl/Alt/Break from the DOS prompt or Ctrl/Alt/Break from any program. Select "Message tasks." On the next menu, select "Start or start saving messages." On this menu, select "Start saving messages" (Fig. 14-3). On the next menu enter the file name or the name of the DOS device to which you wish the log file directed (Fig. 14-4). You can, if you wish, specify the printer device (PRN) and direct the log output to a printer.

You can also use the menu to terminate the use of the log file. At the main menu select "Message tasks." On the next option screen select "Start or stop saving messages." On the next menu, select "Stop saving messages."

To resume the saving of messages, select "Message tasks" from the main menu. Then select "Start or stop saving messages." On the next menu select

```
                                                        PC LAN PROGRAM

              Start or Stop Saving Messages

  1. Start saving messages

  2. Stop saving messages

  1  Choice




  Enter - Continue                      F1 - Help
  Ctrl-Home - Return to Main Menu       Esc - Previous menu
```

Fig. 14-3. Starting to create a log file.

"Start saving messages." *PC Network* will then display the current file name for the log file or DOS device used. Edit this if you wish, then press Enter.

The log file can be displayed or printed as any other disk file. From the main menu, select "Message tasks." On the next menu select "View received messages." Then use the F6 key at any time to view the oldest message in the log file (Fig. 14-5). The F7 key will append the current screen message to the log file. Viewing a message removes the message from the log file. You can also, of course, view the log file with the TYPE command or any editor. The full list of function keys available with this view screen is shown in Table 14-1.

If you wish the use of the log file as a permanent part of your configuration, save the configuration after defining the log file. This will save the current log file definition as a NET LOG command in the AUTOEXEC.BAT file and will initiate the use of this log file each time the network is started.

Once you have defined a log file, it remains in effect (unless refined or terminated) for the duration of the session. If you start another session, you must define the log file again unless the configuration was saved as a part of the AUTOEXEC.BAT file.

You can display the status of the log file using the NET LOG command as:

C > NET LOG < Enter >

This will display a report on the log, showing the status of the log file (whether log activity is on or off) and the name of the log file (see Fig. 14-6). This does not display log file messages, or even an indication if there are messages waiting. It only tells you a log file is active and the name of the file.

You cannot get this display from the *PC LAN* menus, but if you are already in the menus the F2 key will let you enter the NET LOG command. (The NET part of the command will be displayed automatically. You enter LOG following NET.)

Using Buffers

If you do not use a log file and your configuration is a server or messenger,

```
                                                        PC LAN PROGRAM
                     Start or Stop Saving Messages

  1. Start saving messages

  2. Stop saving messages


  1   Choice

  Save messages in filename or DOS device
  CARL.LOG




  Tab - Cursor to next field
  Enter - Save messages                  F1 - Help
  Esc - Previous menu                    Ctrl-Home - Return to Main Menu
```

Fig. 14-4. Naming a log file.

```
MESSAGE FROM SANDYT TO SERVER ON 09/12/86 AT 13:06          PC LAN PROGRAM
                         View Messages

Press F3 to view waiting messages
Press F6 to view next saved messages
_____

i need the printer




_____
Esc - Previous menu or Exit              Ctrl-Home - Return to Main Menu
Ctrl-PgUp - Delete saved message         Ctrl-PgDn - Erase viewed message
F1 HELP/MORE KEYS    F2 COMMAND LINE      F3VIEW NEXT WAITING F4 SEND MESSAGE
F5 VIEW FIRST SAVED F6 VIEW NEXT SAVED    F7 SAVE MESSAGE      F8 PRINT MESSAGE
```

Fig. 14-5. Receiving a message.

Table 14-1. Function Keys Available for the View Screen.

Key	Operation
F1	Help screen (displays this information).
F2	Switch to command mode.
F3	View the earliest message in the message buffer and delete it from the buffer. You can save it to the log file by pressing <F7> before deleting it.
F4	Toggle between View and Send screens. Useful for replying to a message you have just received.
F5	View the first message in the log file.
F6	View the next message in the log file.
F7	Append message on the screen to the log file. If you do not have a log file, you can use <F2> to create one.
F8	Copy the message on the screen to the printer.

```
C:\>net log

Status       Name of Log File

ON           C:\SERVER.LOG

Command completed successfully

C:\>
```

Fig. 14-6. Examining the log file status.

incoming messages can be viewed immediately by using the Ctrl/Alt/Break keys or they can be saved to a buffer using the Ctrl/Break keys. The size of this buffer is defined by the MBI startup parameter, and defaults to 1750 bytes. This will hold several one-line messages, or one message of 1600 characters. If a sender sends a message that overflows the receiver's buffer, the sender gets an error message. The receiver does not get any message or any indication of what has happened. The moral is to use buffers carefully so you do not overflow. Read incoming messages often to keep the buffer clear.

As you read each message in the buffer it is deleted. Displayed messages can be printed with the F8 key. Remember that the buffer is kept only in the computer memory. If the computer is turned off and back on or rebooted, the messages in the buffer are lost. Messages sent to a log file, in contrast, remain intact if the computer is turned off and back on or rebooted.

Note: With some application programs that use the screen in a graphic mode, there will be no message screen when an incoming message is received. The message is stored in the buffer, however, and can be viewed using *PC*

LAN. If messages are waiting in the buffer, the *PC LAN* main menu will indicate this and the number of messages waiting.

USING ADDITIONAL NAMES

Sometimes you may wish to define a second name or alias to apply to the current session. This is most useful in assigning a server name to a server. For example, if Tom is using a server, SERVER1, as a workstation, he may wish to assign the name TOM to the server as well, permitting him to receive messages addressed to TOM or SERVER1. Additional names can be defined either from the menu or with the NET NAME command. Only one alias can be defined at a time.

As an example, suppose the role of the server operator is rotated among several workstation users. Whoever is operator for the day has the alias of OP. If someone needs a special paper in the printer, a message is sent to OP. Whoever has the alias for the day would then receive the message and could act on it.

Defining Aliases with a Command

To define an additional session name for a system, use the NET NAME command as:

C > NET NAME *session__name* < Enter >

For example:

C > NET NAME Tom < Enter >

This would assign "TOM" as an additional session name on the system where the command was issued.

To get a report of current names in use, use the NET NAME command with no parameter. Only one alias can be defined at a time.

Defining Aliases with the Menu

You can also use the *PC LAN* menu to define an alias. Display the main menu, then select "Message tasks." On the next menu select "Start or stop receiving messages for another name." Select "Start receiving messages for another name" on the next menu (Fig. 14-7). On the next screen, fill in the name you wish to use (Fig. 14-8).

To get a report on current names in use, select "Message tasks," then "Display names which can receive messages at your computer." Only one alias can be defined at a time.

```
                                                       PC LAN PROGRAM
            Receiving Messages for Another Name

  1. Start receiving for another name

  2. Stop receiving for another name


  1  Choice








  Enter - Continue                     F1 - Help
  Ctrl-Home - Return to Main Menu      Esc - Previous menu
```

Fig. 14-7. Starting to define an alias.

FORWARDING MESSAGES

It is nice, at times, to be able to forward messages addressed to one computer to another computer. For example, Bill may be a server operator and normally at SERVER1, but today he is helping Bob at the workstation BOB. Bill wants to temporarily forward messages addressed to SERVER1 to Bob's workstation (BOB). In this way, users do not have to keep track of where he is. This can be done from the menu or with the NET FORWARD command.

The request is made only on the forwarding computer. For example, suppose Bill is a server operator with an alias BILL and wants to forward his messages addressed to the server (BILL) to Bob's computer. If the forwarding computer has an alias (SERVER1 is also BILL), only the messages for the specified name are forwarded. To forward for both SERVER1 and BILL, you would need to issue the command for both SERVER1 and BILL.

When you make a forwarding request on the forwarding computer (SERVER1), it sends a message to the destination computer (BOB) to add the new name (BILL) to its list of names. If the request is successful, the forwarding computer removes the name (BILL) from its list of active names.

To forward messages using the command mode, use the following command:

C > NET FORWARD *forwarding destination* < Enter >

where:

> *forwarding* = session name of forwarding machine
> *destination* = session name of destination machine

For example:

C > NET FORWARD BILL BOB < Enter >

```
                                                         PC LAN PROGRAM
                   Receiving Messages for Another Name

   1. Start receiving for another name

   2. Stop receiving for another name


   1  Choice

   Start receiving messages for:
   CARL




   Tab - Cursor to next field
   Enter - Continue              F1 - Help
   Esc - Previous menu           Ctrl-Home - Return to Main Menu
```

Fig. 14-8. Naming an alias.

```
                                                    PC LAN PROGRAM
              Start or Stop Forwarding Messages

   1. Start forwarding messages

   2. Stop forwarding messages


   1  Choice






   Enter - Continue                     F1 - Help
   Ctrl-Home - Return to Main Menu      Esc - Previous menu
```

Fig. 14-9. Starting to forward messages.

To initiate forwarding from a menu, first select "Message tasks" from the menu. On the next menu select "Start or stop forwarding messages." On the next (Fig. 14-9), select "Start forwarding messages." On the remainder of this form (Fig. 14-10), fill in the name of the forwarding computer and the destination computer. Press Enter.

Once a message is put on the network for any session name, it can be claimed by any computer using that session name (or that name as an alias). Forwarding remains in effect until the destination computer removes the name from its table or is turned off. Once the name is removed from the table on the destination computer (or the computer is turned off), the forwarding computer automatically begins reclaiming messages addressed to that name.

If any machine is forwarding messages to a destination machine, the forwarding remains in effect even if the forwarding machine is turned off. In this example, if the server is turned off, Bill's messages will still be directed to Bob's machine.

145

```
                                                         PC LAN PROGRAM
                  Start or Stop Forwarding Messages

     1. Start forwarding messages

     2. Stop forwarding messages


     1  Choice

     Forward messages for (name on your computer)
     BILL

     To (name on another computer)
     BOB




     Tab — Cursor to next field
     Enter — Continue
     Esc — Previous menu              F1 — Help
                                      Ctrl-Home — Return to Main Menu
```

Fig. 14-10. Forwarding messages.

Chapter 15

Special
Networking Commands

T WO SPECIAL COMMANDS ARE AVAILABLE FOR A NETWORK USER. THE NET PAUSE command can be used to temporarily suspend the operation of the network. The PERMIT command is useful for temporarily making any system on the network a dedicated server.

SUSPENDING NETWORK OPERATION

There are times when you may wish to suspend temporarily the operation of a computer on the network. Suspending a computer on the network does not release memory space currently being used for the network software, nor is there any loss of network name assignments or configuration information. Network suspension temporarily withdraws offers to share or use network resources. Tables and parameter data that control current offers remain with the network software in memory.

When would you wish to suspend network operation on a computer? Here are some typical applications:

1. You wish to use a command on the server machine that is not available when the network is operational. (Examples: BACKUP, CHKDSK)

2. You wish to use the floppy disk as Drive A on a computer (for backing up some data, for example), but you have already assigned Drive

A as a virtual disk drive for network use. Suspending the network permits you to use Drive A on your computer again.

3. As a user at a workstation, you are working on a very important program that uses no network resources and you do not wish to be interrupted with network messages.

4. As server you are doing some printing on a laser printer and you need to see the page image immediately and frequently for a project on which you are working. You can temporarily suspend the printer sharing and use the printer as a local printer, bypassing the print queue.

5. You are a server operator and need to change the paper or ribbon on a printer. You can suspend the printer operation while you make the changes.

6. You are a server operator and need to take a dump of a screen image. You can suspend the printer operation, make the dump, and then restore printer operation.

Suspension of network operation on a computer refers to the suspension of a particular type of activity. There are five types of network activities that can be suspended:

DRDR—Your machine's use of directories on another computer on the network (disk redirection).

PRDR—Your machine's use of the network print queue (print redirection).

PRT—Your machine's transfer of files from the print queue to a printer on your machine (printing).

MSG—(Messenger only) Incoming messages.

RCV—(Receiver only) Incoming messages.

SRV—(Server only) All network requests.

· You cannot suspend the use of a particular disk directory or device. Suspension always refers to broad categories. A suspension is only in effect for the duration of the session. If you initiate a suspension and then shut your network down, the suspension is not saved. When you start the network again, the suspension will not be in effect. This can create some interesting surprises. For example, suppose a printer is misbehaving late Friday. You have suspended the printer to work on the printer, then shut the network down. On Monday, you start the network with several jobs in the print queue that have been waiting for the printer. The printer is still misbehaving and the suspension is no longer in effect. In the next chapter you will see some ways to control this kind of situation.

Let us look at each of these categories more specifically.

Disk Redirection (DRDR)

Disk redirection refers to the suspension of the use of the virtual directories of the server on a user machine in the network. When this suspension has been issued on a user machine, the user machine no longer has the use of server directories available through the network. All assignments defined with the NET USE command are suspended, except for printer requests.

Once you have initiated this type of suspension, all virtual disk assignments temporarily revert to their normal local assignments. For example, suppose you used a NET USE command at a workstation to assign a directory on the network server as Disk Drive A on your local workstation. After the NET USE command, the local disk drive would no longer be accessible, as Drive A is mapped to a server directory. Then you discover you need to copy a file to a diskette on the local disk drive, which was formerly Drive A. Once this type of suspension is initiated, Drive A refers again (temporarily) to the floppy disk drive on the user's machine and the copy could be made.

Print Redirection (PRDR)

Print redirection refers to the suspension of the process of redirecting print requests through the network to the network print queue. Once this suspension is initiated on a user machine, print requests that would normally be directed through the network will instead be directed to the local printer. This suspends printer redirection defined with a NET USE command. Although printer and disk redirection on a user machine are both defined with a NET USE command, each type of redirection can be suspended separately.

If you are using a server machine, this type of redirection is a little different. The printer in this case is both the local printer and the network printer. If you suspend print redirection on a server, the server printer temporarily becomes a local printer. As a result, you will also suspend the print background program and the transfer of any print requests from the print queue to the printer. Using this alternative, you can suspend output from the queue and use the printer temporarily for screen dumps.

The Print Background Program (PRT)

When a print request is directed to a network printer, there are two steps. The first step is the transfer of the print image to a print queue. The second step is the actual printing of the image from the queue by a background print program.

In a PRDR suspension, you suspend the transfer of print requests to the queue, transferring the requests instead to a local printer. In a PRT-type suspension, you are suspending the transfer of printing from the queue to a specific printer or to all printers on a server using that queue. The PRT suspension is particularly useful if you need to make adjustments on a printer (change the ribbon or paper).

With a PRT-type request, the queue is not affected. Even though the printing is suspended, jobs will still accumulate in the queue waiting for the print function to be reinstated. If you suspend only a single printer, any jobs in the queue directed to other printers will continue to be printed.

If you initiated the suspension while a job is printing, the printing will be terminated immediately, but the job will not be removed from the queue. When the printing function is resumed, the job will be printed again from the beginning.

If you initiate a print redirection suspension (PRDR) on a server, a suspension will also be initiated for the printer (PRT) for all network requests, as the printer will revert to a local printer.

Message Reception (RCV or MSG)

MSG or RCV suspension refers to the suspension of message reception on a user machine. If you use a command mode to specify the type of suspension, you must specify the configuration of the user machine (RCV or MSG). If you use the menu mode to suspend, it is not necessary to know the configuration.

While message reception is suspended, you can still use any other functions on your machine that relate to message handling. The Send and View screens are still available and can be used to send messages or view messages received earlier. You can still add an alias name, and messages that should be forwarded will continue to be forwarded.

Server Activity (SRV)

When SRV suspension is initiated on a server, all network activity on the server is suspended. It suspends the use of server directories on the network (directories that are shared), the use of the print queue, and all incoming messages.

Unlike other suspensions, this is a rather dramatic type of suspension which has serious consequences. You should always check with all users on the network before initiating this type of suspension. Because of the nature of this type of suspension, *PC LAN* will not allow you to use it if any file is open on a directory shared with the network. If you try to suspend with the files open, you will get a network error message informing you that files are open.

STARTING AND TERMINATING SUSPENSIONS

As with other network operations, you can start and stop suspensions using either the menu mode or the command mode.

To use the menu mode, start from the main menu as with any other command:

1. Display the main menu using the Ctrl/Alt/Break key from an application program or the NET command or Ctrl/Alt/Break keys from the DOS prompt.

2. From the main menu, select "Pause and continue tasks." This will give a full list of the suspension functions available with your particular configuration (see Fig. 15-1).

```
                                                    PC LAN PROGRAM
                      Pause and Continue Tasks

1. Pause or continue using network disks and directories

2. Pause or continue using network printers

3. Pause or continue receiving messages


1  Choice




Enter - Continue                 F1 - Help
Ctrl-Home - Return to Main Menu   Esc - Previous menu
```

Fig. 15-1. Starting a suspension.

3. Select the desired function.

4. If you make any selection other than "Pause or continue printing files," you will get another menu with two options: "Pause" or "Continue" (Fig. 15-2). Select the desired option. With the "Pause or continue printing files" option, you will get an additional menu that asks if you wish to pause or continue a specific printer or all printers.

5. Once the action is initiated, you will get a message confirming the action, or an error message.

If you wish to restore a suspension, use the same menus and select the "Continue" option instead of the "Pause" option.

To initiate a suspension using the command mode, use the NET PAUSE command in the following form:

C> NET PAUSE *suspension_type* <Enter>

```
                                                    PC LAN PROGRAM
              Pause or Continue Using Network Disks And Directories

         1. Pause using network disks and directories

         2. Continue using network disks and directories


         1  Choice







         Enter - Continue                      F1 - Help
         Ctrl-Home - Return to Main Menu       Esc - Previous menu
```

Fig. 15-2. Suspending access to network disks.

where *suspension__type* is the type of suspension desired. For example, to suspend all printers on a server you would use the following command:

C> NET PAUSE PRT <Enter>

Note: You can also use PRINT for this type of suspension type.

C> NET PAUSE PRT=LPT1 <Enter>

To restore the network function (and terminate the suspension), use the NET CONTINUE command. As with NET PAUSE, you must also specify the type of suspension to restore:

C> NET CONTINUE PRT <Enter>

CREATING TEMPORARY SERVERS

Any user on the network can temporarily make their machine a type server using the PERMIT command. As you can imagine, this is a very powerful command. It has both advantages and disadvantages.

There also are many applications in which you might wish to use the PERMIT command. Here are a few examples:

1. You need to transfer a file to another user on the network. Using PERMIT to share the directory that contains the file permits the user to transfer the file to his or her local machine using a COPY command.

2. You need to access a file on a workstation that does not have a hard disk.

3. You need to maintain the security of a particular data file, and do not wish to place it on a server. The PERMIT command makes it possible to share it with a single user, whom you specify, and no other users on the network.

With normal resource sharing, an offer is made to share the resource using the NET SHARE command on a server. A user accepts the offer using the NET USE command. The NET SHARE command can only be used on a computer configured as a server, and the server must have a hard disk.

The PERMIT command lets any system on the network share a resource (including a workstation), which can then be taken up by a user machine using the NET USE command.

From the user's perspective there is no difference if the resource is offered by a server or another user using the PERMIT command. The user still defines the resource using the NET USE command (or a menu) as though it were from a server.

From the sharer's perspective, however, there are several distinctions between an offer using the PERMIT command and an offer from a server. Let's look at the advantages and disadvantages of the PERMIT command:

Advantages and Disadvantages

The two main advantages are, first, that any user on the network can share a resource, and the user does not need a hard disk. Moreover, the sharing machine does not even need to be running the *PC Local Area Network* software. The only requirement is that it have a network adapter card linking it to the network. The PERMIT command can be issued without *PC LAN* being resident.

There also are a few disadvantages. The sharing machine that issues the PERMIT command is 100-percent dedicated to the network—you cannot use it as a workstation at the same time—and the offer to share can be taken up by only one other machine in the network at a time. In addition, the PERMIT command is not a part of any menu. It must be initiated outside of the menus.

Making an Offer with PERMIT

The PERMIT command is not a part of *PC LAN*. There is no NET PERMIT form of the command, nor is it an option on the menu. PERMIT is a separate program on the *PC LAN* disk. The general form of the PERMIT command is somewhat similar to the NET SHARE command:

C >PERMIT *network_name = path destination_name originator access*
<Enter>

where:

network_name	=	optional network name for the sharer's directory.
path	=	directory to be shared.
destination_name	=	session name of user who is permitted access.
originator	=	a special name for the offering computer.
access	=	the access level permitted.

You must adopt a new name for your system that is used by *destination_name* to access the shared directory. It cannot be the same as the current session name or any other user on the network.

The access levels permitted are the same as those for the NET SHARE command:

R	Read-only access
W	Write to existing files
RW	Read and write access
WC	Write, create and delete files
RWC	Read, write, create and delete files

You may omit the access level if desired, and the command will assume a default value of RWC. The true access level of any file that is offered is controlled using the DOS ATTRIB command or the access level in the PERMIT command, whichever is more restrictive. For example, if you offer a file that is read-only using the PERMIT command, with an RWC access level, the user will only be able to read the file.

As with NET SHARE, you can offer a directory without the network name (short name) and equal sign, permitting the intended user to access the directory by its true path name.

For example, suppose Tom is offering a spreadsheet data file that is on a subdirectory called LOTUS. He offers the directory as DATA, with a read-only access level to the server. His own session name is Tom, so he temporarily uses TOMT as a new session name:

C> PERMIT DATA = C: \ LOTUS SERVER1 TOMT /R < Enter>

Tom must use a new name for his system in the PERMIT command that is not the same as his session name. If the command does not work, be sure the PERMIT.COM file is on the current workstation directory, you are not using your current session name, and the syntax is correct. Remember that PERMIT functions much as any DOS external command and is separate from the network programs. It is not necessary for the workstation to be using *PC LAN*, but an adapter card must be installed and the workstation connected to a MAU.

Once the offer is made, Tom's computer will be a dedicated server. Tom will not be able to use the system for anything until the PERMIT command is terminated.

You can also use an asterisk for the *destination_name* to specify that the offer to share can be taken up by any user. In this case, the first user to take up the offer to share will be permitted to use the resource.

Taking Up the Offer

The user takes up the offer with a NET USE command or through the use of the *PC LAN* menus. In either case, it is just as though the resource were offered from a server.

If the command mode is selected:

```
C> NET USE G: \ \TOMT\DATA <Enter>
```

This will enable the server to access any files on Tom's \LOTUS directory using the Drive G designator. A colon must follow the designator, and a double slash must precede the temporary session name of the sharing computer. Once the server has taken up the offer and is using the resource, Tom will see a message that the directory is in use. The normal DOS prompt will not be on Tom's computer until the offer is terminated.

If the menu mode is selected, it is again identical to using a resource from a server (Chapter 13). From the main menu select "Disk or directory tasks." On the next menu select "Start or stop using a network disk or directory." Select "Start using a network disk or directory" on the next menu. Fill in the form and press Enter.

Terminating

If a user wishes to terminate the offer, it is done as if it were from a server. Either the command mode or menu mode can be used. From the command mode, the NET USE command is used with the name of the drive designator and a /D:

```
C> NET USE G: /D <Enter>
```

To use the main menu, from the main menu select "Disk or directory tasks." On the next menu select "Start or stop using a network disk or directory." Select "Stop using a network disk or directory" on the next menu. Fill in the form and press Enter.

In our example, the server is the user. Once the server is through with Tom's directory, the server enters:

```
C>NET USE G: /D
```

This terminates the PERMIT command and returns Tom's computer to local use. (As an experiment, try this and terminate the use of the G directory from the G directory. You will find it functions correctly. The use is terminated, the local workstation returned to the user, and the server gets a message. What would you expect the server message to say?)

From the view of the system sharing the resource, there is not much that can be done after PERMIT is issued. The sharing system is dedicated to the user using the resource. If the user is not logged onto the network or has not accepted the offer to use the resource, the sharing system waits patiently until the offer to share is accepted. Once the user accepts the offer and then terminates the use of the resource, the PERMIT command terminates and the sharing computer returns to the DOS prompt, ready to be used again.

If you have issued a PERMIT command on a workstation and then decide you do not wish to share the resource, you can interrupt and terminate the PERMIT command. It is only necessary to press the Ctrl/Break keys. This returns the workstation to the DOS prompt and terminates the PERMIT command and the offer to share. If you wish to share the resource again, you must issue another PERMIT command. If the user had already issued a NET USE command, he (or she) will need to delete the use of the resource and then issue another NET USE command after PERMIT has been issued again.

Chapter 16

Managing
Network Printers

THIS CHAPTER WILL GIVE YOU AN INTRODUCTION TO MANAGING PRINTers on a network. You will learn how the print spool works, how to control the print queue, and how to use separator sheets.

The only configuration that can support a printer for network use is the server configuration. To use the printer as a network device, the printer must first be offered to the network (using the NET SHARE command). Users can then accept the offer to use the printer by using the NET USE command. The commands to share and use the printer can be saved as a permanent part of the AUTOEXEC.BAT file, automatically configuring the network when each computer is started so the printer is available to each user.

The print process on the network is actually divided into two phases (Fig. 16-1). In the first, the data to be printed is accepted by the server and used to create a print image file. As each file is created, it is saved as a PQ*xxx*.SPL file on the \NETWORK directory, where *xxx* is a number from 000-999. This is the print queue. Up to 100 files can be created and saved, waiting for printer availability.

A record of the file to print is also stored in the file \NETWORK\PQ.SPL. This file is actually a table that contains the status information of each file in the print queue. There must be enough room on the hard disk for the files of all jobs waiting to be printed.

In the second phase, each job is transferred in turn from the print queue to the appropriate printer. This is done by a background print program (the print manager program) that is a part of *PC LAN*. (The background program

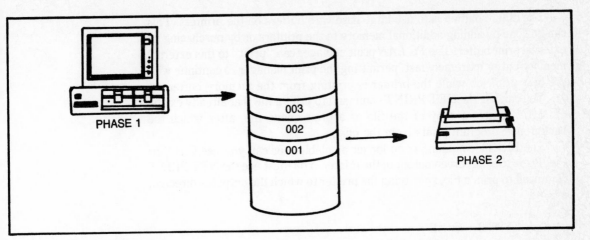

Fig. 16-1. The two print phases.

is on the disk as \NETWORK\PSPRINT.EXE.) This is done so efficiently that printing continues on the server while the server is doing other work (such as supporting an application program) in the foreground.

Both the print program and application program appear to work at the same time. The application program is the foreground program; that is, visible to the user. The printing program is a background program, operating invisibly to the user. The startup TSI parameter determines how the computer divides the clock cycles between the application program and the print program.

If you are printing to a network printer from a word processor or spreadsheet program, you actually "print" to a file in the print queue, which is then printed on the printer by the background program.

If you turn the server off and then back on (restarting the network), the print queue remains intact, because it is stored on disk. Printing continues at the beginning of the next job. If a job was printing when the server went down, printing starts at the beginning of the job that was printing.

There may be several printers connected to a server. You may share any of them, all of them, or none of them with the network. Once a printer is shared with the network, it is no longer a local printer. Any local printing will be directed through the print queue automatically.

You may share several printers on the server, but there is always only one print queue. If there are several jobs in the queue waiting for different printers, there will only be one printer printing at a time. Each job in the queue will go to the appropriate printer in turn, but only one job will be printed at a time. If this is a problem, there are two possible solutions.

The first solution is to set up two or more servers, putting the network printers on different servers. In this way you will have multiple queues and two or more printers can print at once.

The other solution is to use large hardware buffers on the printers. This can be done by adding additional memory to the printers or by purchasing an external print buffer. The *PC LAN* print manager can "print" to this external memory buffer extremely fast, permitting the print manager to continue with the next print job while the printer is printing from the memory buffer.

You can use the NET PRINT command to print a file that already exists. *PC LAN* creates a copy of the file as a print queue file, after which the background program prints from the queue.

The PRINT command is no longer available, nor can you use Ctrl/P or Ctrl/PrtSc to send screen output to the printer. You must use the NET PRINT command to print a file, specifying the printer to which the output is directed, as:

```
C > NET PRINT *.doc lpt1
```

INITIALIZING AND STARTUP PARAMETERS

Printers vary widely, and how they are supported by the computer varies, too. In some cases you may wish to send certain codes to a printer before the print manager is started, to initialize the printer. One alternative is to create a short BASIC program that sends these codes to the printer, making the last statement of the BASIC program a SYSTEM statement. A command line is then added in AUTOEXEC.BAT before the startup commands for the network, such as:

```
BASICA progname
```

where *progname* is the name of your BASIC program. If a suitable compiler is available, you could convert the program into an EXE file and eliminate the extra time needed to load BASICA.COM. This technique is a quick way to set fonts, margins, or whatever is necessary before the network and print manager are started (the print manager starts automatically when the network is started).

Several startup parameters affect printer operation. You may wish to experiment with each of these to find the most efficient values for your system.

REQ: Server Requests

The REQ parameter defines the number of server requests the server can process at one time. The value can be 1 to 3, with a default value of 2. If the server is dedicated, the value of 1 should not be used. If the server is very busy, use a value of 3.

RQB: Network Transmission Buffer Size

RQB is the size of the buffer used for transferring network data to the queue when printing. The default value is 8K. If server memory is available, you might increase this to 16K to reduce disk activity.

TSI: Server Time Allocation

The computer processor time is divided between the foreground tasks (the application program) and background tasks (processing network requests and printing). The TSI value controls how this time is divided. The value is a two-digit number. The first digit determines how many timer ticks to allocate for foreground tasks before they are stopped, while the second defines the number of timer ticks for the background tasks before they are stopped. Normally there are 18.2 ticks per second; each tick is about 54.945 milliseconds. The following table can be used to correlate TSI values to timer ticks:

TSI value	Timer ticks
0	1
1	2
2	3
3	5
4	7
5	11
6	15
7	21
8	28
9	36

To specify a TSI, use two of the above TSI values to determine how the clock cycles are split. The TSI defaults to a value of 54, which represents the relationship of 5 foreground intervals or 11 timer ticks (604.395 milliseconds), to 4 background intervals or 7 timer ticks (384.615 milliseconds). With a TSI value of 00, background tasks will always have priority and foreground tasks will only run if there are no background tasks. Use a 00 value if the printer is not being shared. If you are sharing a printer, try starting with a TSI value of 26.

PRB: Print Buffer

This defines the size of the buffer used to transfer data from the print queue to the printer. The default value is 512 bytes. The server will require twice the value you specify for PRB in memory space. If you have sufficient memory available, increase this value to 2K. This will reduce disk activity and show noticeable speed improvement with higher-speed printers.

PCx: Print Count

PCx defines the number of characters sent to the print buffer in a single operation, with x defining the number of the printer (2 = LPT2). This will normally only need to be changed for a faster printer, with normal values ranging from 100-200. Change PCx in increments of 50 only. The larger the value, the faster the printer will print. The smaller the number, the better the foreground response.

MANAGING THE PRINT QUEUE

You can also manage the print queue, changing the order in which the jobs will print and changing the status of jobs. This can only be done from the menu, as there is no command that controls the queue. You may also use this menu selection to examine the status of the print queue.

To examine the print queue, display the main menu and select "Print queue tasks." On the next menu (Fig. 16-2), select "Check or change print queue tasks on your computer." You will then see a display similar to that in Fig.

```
                    Print Queue Tasks                    PC LAN PROGRAM

    1. Check or change print queue on your computer

    2. Check print queue on another computer

    3. Start or stop printing a separator page


    1  Choice






    Enter - Continue                    F1 - Help
    Ctrl-Home - Return to Main Menu      Esc - Previous menu
```

Fig. 16-2. Beginning to check the print queue.

```
                                                         PC LAN PROGRAM
                   Check or Change the Print Queue

1. Update queue    ID  User Name      Size    Device    Status
                                  -- Start of Queue --
2. Hold            008 SERVER                  LPT1      SPOOLING
                                  --  End of Queue --
3. Release

4. Cancel

5. Print next

6. Print now


1  Choice


  and  - Select file                 PgUp and PgDn - Scroll List
       Enter - Change queue                 F1 - Help
       Ctrl-Home - Return to Main Menu       Esc - Previous menu
```

Fig. 16-3. Viewing the print queue.

16-3. Each job has a status field that describes the present status of the job. There are eight possible status values:

PRINTING—The computer has begun transferring the data from the queue file to the printer.

HELD—The job has been flagged to be held. Jobs that are held retain their position in the queue, but are not printed until released.

WAITING—The job is not held, but is not printing, and is waiting for printer time.

CANCELLED—This is a very temporary status. The job has been printed, but not removed from the queue yet. The job will probably be gone the next time the status is displayed. If the job was printing and the printing terminated, the status will return to waiting status.

PAUSED—This indicates a job is directed to a printer that is currently paused.

SPOOLING—The file is being sent to the queue.

PRINTER ERROR—An attempt was made to print the file, but the request was unsuccessful. Probably the printer was not ready.

PRINT FILE ERROR—The print manager attempted to print a file that was no longer in the queue.

You can use the same menu that shows the status of the print queue to change the status of jobs in the print queue or the order of the jobs. When the status screen is displayed, you will see one line of the status screen (one job) highlighted. You can select any of the six options on the left of the screen to control the one job that is highlighted. You can use the up and down arrows to move the highlighting to other jobs. Here is a brief description of each of the options:

HOLD—The job will remain in the queue, continuing to move to the top of the queue as other jobs are printed. Once the job is at the top of the queue, it is not printed but remains at the top of the queue. The next job not held is printed.

RELEASE—Converts the status of a held job to printing, if it is at the top of the queue, and to waiting if it is anywhere else in the queue.

CANCEL—Removes the job from the queue if it is printing or waiting to print. If printing, the printing for the job is terminated.

PRINT NEXT—Takes the selected job and moves it to the top of the queue, where it is printed next. A held job will not be printed, but will be moved in the queue.

PRINT NOW—Cancel whatever is printing and print this job. The job that is printing now will be printed next (from the beginning again).

PRINT NOW is a rather strong option and should be used only if absolutely necessary. In most cases, if an immediate output is desired you should select PRINT NEXT.

USING NET PAUSE

The NET PAUSE command provides a method of temporarily suspending output to the printer or recovering the use of the network printer as a local printer. This was more fully discussed in the last chapter, and should be referred to as a review.

FORCING PRINTING

In some cases you may try to print a job from an application program only to discover the job goes to the print queue but does not print immediately. To force the print, you must exit the application program. A good example of this is trying to print a spreadsheet from *Lotus 1-2-3*. The application program does not put an end-of-file indicator as the last character when the file is sent to the print queue. The result is that print requests continue to pile up in the print queue, eventually even exhausting the available disk space.

To prevent print requests from accumulating in this manner, follow this simple procedure: After the print job has been sent to the queue, press Ctrl/Alt/PrtSc. This will force an end-of-file into the print queue, and the printing will start. Be sure not to press the keys too soon, or you will split your hard copy.

THE SEPARATOR PAGE

PC LAN permits you to define a separator page that is used as a header page when printing each job. The use of the separator page is optional, but highly advisable. The separator page serves two functions. It resets the printer from any control settings of the previous job (such as compressed print), and it marks the beginning of each job in the printout.

The separator page is defined by a file. The file can be created and edited with any editor or word processor in the non-document mode. You can turn on the separator page by selecting the file with the NET SEPARATOR command or, as with other commands, by using the menu.

To get you started the network comes with a sample separator page file called \NETWORK\PQ.SEP (Fig. 16-4). This will work on an IBM color printer and can be modified for other printers using any editor or a word processor in the nondocument mode. An example separator page using PQ.SEP is shown in Fig. 16-5. Another example separator file, PQ.OEM (Fig. 16-6), is a skeleton file that can be built up to support almost any printer.

To initiate the use of the separator page using the command mode, specify the printer and separator page file as:

C > NET SEPARATOR LPT1 \NETWORK\PQ.SEP   <Enter>

You can discontinue its use by specifying the printer and using the /D option:

C > NET SEPARATOR LPT1 /D   <Enter>

From the main menu, start the use of a separator page by selecting "Print queue tasks." Then select "Start or stop printing a separator page." Select

```
@
@H1B@H32
@H1B@H39
@H1B@H43@H42
@H1B@H46
@H1B@H48
@H1B@H54
@H1B@H57@H00
@H1B@H49@H01
@H1B@H55@H00
@H1B@H6E@H00
@H1B@H2D@H00
@H1B@H37
@H1B@H43@H00@H0B
@H0F@0
@H1B@H30@0
@B@M@LIBM@0
@B@M@LPC LAN@0
@B@M@LPROGRAM@0
@U@H12@L(C) Copyright IBM Corporation 1984,1986@0
@B@H0F@0
@4@S@0
@N@0
@4@M@0
@I@0
@4@H12
@U@0
@4@D@L        @T@0
@E
@H1B@H32
```

Fig. 16-4. Defining a separator page: the PQ.SEP file.

"Start printing a separator page on your printer," then fill in the names of the separator file and printer (Fig. 16-7). You can stop the use of a separator page with the same menus, selecting the stop option on the last menu.

You can use the NET SEPARATOR command with no parameters to determine the status of the use of the separator page.

Once you have defined a separator page it is not necessary to save the configuration. The definition is saved immediately in the \ NET-WORK \ PQ.SPL file (which is the print queue status table), and remains active, even if you stop and restart the network.

You should take the time to create your own separator page, starting with the existing examples and then taking a little creative license. IBM provides over a dozen commands that can be used to create block letters, print the date and time, and do other interesting things. The full list of the command codes is shown in Table 16-1. Be sure, when creating your separator page, to include the proper codes to return the printer to normal print (using *@Hnn*). Study the sample separator pages included in this chapter before designing your own.

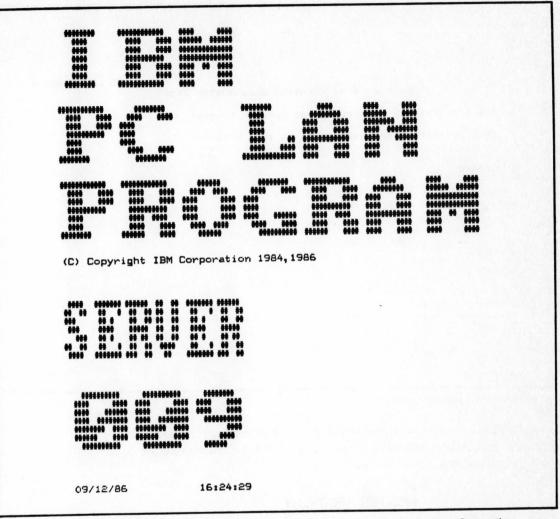

Fig. 16-5. The separator page from the PQ.SEP file. Courtesy of International Business Machines Corporation.

Fig. 16-6. The PQ.OEM file.

```
C:\NETWORK>
@@LIBM PC LAN PROGRAM@O
@4
@B@M@I@O
@U@4
( @N@O
@4
@D@L            @T@O
@E
```

```
                                                      PC LAN PROGRAM
            Start or Stop Printing a Separator Page
   1. Start printing a separator page on your printer

   2. Stop printing a separator page on your printer


   1  Choice
   _
   Name of printer on your computer
   LPT1     (LPT1, LPT2, ...)
   ____




   Enter - Continue                    F1 - Help
   Ctrl-Home - Return to Main Menu      Esc - Previous menu
```

Fig. 16-7. Starting a separator page print.

Note: The date and time printed on the separator page using the @D and @T codes are the dates and times the report is printed, and do not indicate when the request was sent to the queue.

PRINTER RECOVERY

If something happens to the computer during the print cycle, there is very little likelihood of losing the job. The job is not removed from the print queue until it has printed completely. If power is lost or the computer rebooted while the printer is in use, when you restart the network the print will begin from the beginning of the last job. This may be a little inconvenient, but at least you do not lose the job.

If something happens while the printer is paused, when you restart the pause will not be in effect and printing will start immediately. To prevent this if the printer is paused, restart the network with the printer off. Then go into the print queue and adjust it as necessary or use the NET PAUSE command before turning the printer on.

Table 16-1. Separator Codes.

Code	Function
@0	Zero Indicates a hard carriage return. Each carriage return on the separator must be defined explicitly.
@n	Skip *n* lines.
@B	Start the use of block letters.
@D	Print the current date in eight characters.
@E	Eject page. Should be the last code on the page.
@Fxxx	Insert from file *xxx* into separator page printing.
@Hnn	Specify ASCII control character (hexadecimal *nn*).
@I	Print three-digit job number.
@L	Print text that follows.
@M	Start double width (@B must precede).
@N	Print session name for job.
@S	Restore single width (after @M).
@T	Print the time in eight characters.
@U	End use of block letters.

Chapter 17

Managing the
Local Area Network

MANAGING THE LOCAL AREA NETWORK INVOLVES MANY FUNCTIONS: backing up files, ensuring security, choosing and using application programs, and setting up batch files. In this chapter we will look at many of these functions.

HUMAN RESOURCES

Keeping a network operational takes a considerable amount of work. There are four roles involved in network use: the administrator, system integrator, the server operators, and the users. One person may function in two or three of these roles.

Define each of these roles in your network and document the job responsibilities for each as you perceive them in your network. You should also document who has the responsibility for each role. Some people may have more than one role.

The Administrator

The *administrator* (only one administrator for each network.) is responsible for:

- Defining session names that control network access.

- Defining network resource names used by each user on the network.

- Controlling network security.

- Defining application programs supported by the network.

The administrator might or might not also be a network user. None of the job descriptions in the above list require network access.

The System Integrator

The *system integrator* person has the technical responsibility for network support. He or she may be the data processing manager, or perhaps a consultant. Here are some of the responsibilities of the system integrator:

- Works with the administrator, server operators, and users during the planning phase to be sure the network meets the user's needs. Helps define security and back up procedures.

- Installs the network, bringing it up the first time and getting all servers and workstations fully operational.

- Measures the performance of the network against previously defined objective criteria, tuning the network (adjusting startup parameters) as necessary.

- Works with the administrator and server operators to allocate network resources efficiently.

- Works with server operators to respond to error messages and technical problems.

The Server Operator

Each server has a *server operator* responsible for operations on that server. Here are the responsibilities of the server operator:

- Keeping the printers operational.

- Making backups.

- Issuing the network name assignments and passwords for directories on the server and the printer.

- Helping users supported by the server.

- Responding to server messages.

- Creating and editing server batch files.

- Doing preventive maintenance for the server, peripherals, and perhaps other systems in the network.

- Tuning the server for maximum efficiency (adjusting the startup parameters).

In some systems, one of the server operators may also be the administrator.

The Users

The users are those for whom the network exists. The users generally are responsible for their own application programs, tuning their own system, and backing up all files on their local computers. In some cases they may be responsible for the creation of any server batch files needed to support their application.

BACKING UP NETWORK FILES

One of the most important issues that must be addressed by the administrator is the procedure for backing up files on the network. This procedure should be documented and distributed to all users so everyone clearly understands backup responsibilities and procedures. Here are some questions that must be addressed:

1. Who is responsible for each type of backup on the network and how is each backup to be done? Example: The server operator may be responsible for backing up the server, and the local user for backing up the local workstations.

2. How often should each type of backup be done?

3. When should the backups be done? Backing up a server normally requires shutting down the network. The timing of a server backup, then, should be chosen so as to minimize any interference with local users.

4. How many levels of backups are to be saved, and for how long should each backup be saved? For example, when a hard disk is backed up you should not use the same set of disks or the same tape each time. There should be several levels of backups available, rotating the disks and tapes each time a backup is made. This ensures that if something happens to this Friday's backup, you still have the backup you made the previous Friday.

There are several ways to back up a hard disk:

1. You can back up the entire disk.

2. You can back up only the files added or changed since the last backup.

3. You can back up only the files added or changed since a specified date.

4. You can back up only specified directories.

You may wish to use a certain type of back up at certain times and another type of back up at other times.

As a strategy example, you might make the server operators responsible for all backups on the server machines. An incremental backup is made of the server disks each Friday afternoon at 4:00 P.M., of files added or changed during the week. A complete backup of each entire hard disk is made the last day of the month at the end of the day. The backups are stored in separate geographic sites (the manager takes them home) or in a bank vault. Users have the responsibility of backing up all files on their individual machines as necessary.

If you wish to use the DOS BACKUP and RECOVER programs, you will find them somewhat limited. They are slow and do not work with many external media. There are many alternative programs you can use that are more efficient and provide better options. For example, Fifth Generation's *Fastback* is one of the best backup programs for backing up a hard disk to diskettes, backing up 10 megabytes in 8 minutes.

You might also wish to investigate the use of alternative backup hardware, such as streaming tape. If you install the hardware on any server in the network, it can be used to back up any user on the network. Your backup system should be dependable and reliable. There is nothing more frustrating than backing up files to a tape or cartridge unit that is used only for backup (perhaps only once a week) and to then discover on a recovery attempt that the system cannot recover.

Both the backing up and recovery procedures should be tested before they are released for use as standard procedures. Create backup and recovery batch files to control procedures so there is confidence that all files that should be backed up are actually backed up each time the procedures are executed.

PREVENTIVE MAINTENANCE

To minimize unpredictable down time someone should be assigned to do preventive maintenance on servers, peripherals (printers), and workstations. In most cases this will be the responsibility of the server operator. Some general preventive maintenance rules include:

1. Periodically check air flow around each piece of equipment. Be sure

each fan is working and that the flow of air needed for cooling is not blocked. Be sure no equipment is overheated or unusually noisy.

2. Monitor temperature and environment around each system. No one should smoke near the computer, as the smoke particles can damage diskettes and hard disks.

3. Periodically vacuum the printers and equipment to remove particles and dust.

4. Be sure diskette drive heads are kept clean. Whether the heads should be cleaned, and how often, depends upon the environment and other factors.

5. Be sure all equipment is secure. Vibration and shock is particularly damaging to hard disks.

6. Keep floppy disks in dust-free containers.

Whoever has the responsibility for preventive maintenance should keep a log of all work performed on each machine.

BATCH FILES REVISITED

Batch files are very important, as they dramatically simplify the use of the system. Two types of batch files are of particular interest to the server operator and users: the startup files activated during boot-up, and the batch files used to start application programs.

The Startup Batch Files

In any DOS system, AUTOEXEC.BAT is called automatically by the operating system during boot-up. In the case of a DOS system on *PC LAN*, AUTOEXEC.BAT is used to start the network and defines the network configuration. You can also include additional DOS commands at the beginning of the AUTOEXEC.BAT file that will be executed before the network is started. The AUTOEXEC.BAT batch file, on completion, should call AUTOUSER.BAT, which generally contains the commands that were formerly a part of AUTOEXEC.BAT when the network was not in use.

You will want to define both AUTOEXEC.BAT and AUTOUSER.BAT carefully. AUTOEXEC.BAT is created automatically when you save the configuration. You should edit this file to include any commands that should be executed before the network is started. Resident programs that are loaded may be loaded before or after the network software, depending on the requirements of the program.

The PATH command is used in both AUTOEXEC.BAT and AUTOUSER.BAT to define the directories that will be searched for executable files. For example, if you have executed the command:

C > PATH C:\;C:\NETWORK   <Enter>

and then enter the command:

C > CHKDSK C: <Enter>

DOS will first try to find the CHKDSK program on the current directory. If this fails, DOS will search the root directory on Drive C. If this fails, the C:\NETWORK directory will be searched. Only if this fails will a message be displayed that DOS cannot find the program. PATH is used to define both the directories to search and the order in which to search the directories. The current directory is always searched first, even though it is not specified in the command.

The search only applies to COM, EXE and BAT file extensions. It will not work for overlay or data files. Normally it is not necessary to put a PATH command in the AUTOEXEC.BAT file, because when you save a network configuration a PATH command is saved with the configuration to set up the network properly. You will, however, need to put the proper PATH command in the AUTOUSER.BAT file.

The PROMPT command can be used to define the DOS prompt used for all commands on the system. The default prompt is the disk drive designator and a greater-than symbol. You will probably wish to change this by adding the PROMPT command to the AUTOUSER.BAT file. You can include the directory name in the prompt by using:

C > PROMPT pg   <Enter>

If you would like to have the date and time in the prompt line, you might use:

C > PROMPT da thhh$a paga

Another interesting variation will put the date and directory at the top of the screen in inverse video:

C > PROMPT $e[s$e[1;1H$e[k $e[7m $t $d $p $e[0m$e[ung

If you wish to be more creative and try other variations, look up the parameter options in your DOS manual in the command description.

175

Other Batch Files

When a user wishes to start an application, the environment for the application must be set up. This setup often requires the use of directories on a network server. There are two basic philosophies on requesting to use network resources:

1. When the workstation is started, request to use everything that might possibly be used. Put all the NET USE commands as a part of the AUTOEXEC.BAT file and issue the appropriate PATH and APPEND commands to make all directories accessible.

2. When the workstation is started, minimize the requests. Put the appropriate requests (NET USE commands, PATH, and APPEND commands) in the batch file that starts a particular application. The batch file must also save the current environment to a batch file which is executed on leaving the application environment. Figure 17-1 shows an example. The batch file should begin by seeing if the offer has already been made to use the resource. This is done by trying to find a file on the shared directory. If this fails, the request is made to use the resource.

Each method has advantages and disadvantages. How the network is used will determine which is more appropriate.

```
echo off
if exist g:\batch\*.* goto valid
rem when no files in g:\batch, it needs a NET USE
net use g:\\SERVER1\APPS > nul
if errorlevel 1 goto problem
:valid
:      Make a local copy of cleansav.bat
copy g:\batch\cleansave.bat > nul
:      Build SAVEPATH.BAT to restore environment later
echo echo off > savepath.bat
path > > savepath.bat
append > > savepath.bat
echo net use g: /d > > savepath.bat
echo if not errorlevel 1 echo DRIVE G deleted > > savepath.bat
echo cleansave.bat > > savepath.bat
environment for application
: path G:\APPS\WP\MW;G:\APPS\MSTOOLS;G:APPS\NETWORK;G:\APPS\DOS
append N:\PROFILES
MW %1
savepath
goto end
:Problem
rem Unable to execute Microsoft Word on Server
:end
```

Fig. 17-1. A batch file for an application program.

The NETPATH File. If you use the Installation Aid to install the network, that aid creates a NETPATH batch file for each user. This resets the proper path for the user to access the public directory. The NETPATH command can be used after an application program has executed to restore the proper path command.

SECURITY

What level of network security is needed, and how should it be implemented?

The most secure type of system is the single-user floppy disk system. When you are through with the computer you simply remove the disk and lock it in a drawer, put it in a safe at the bank, or take it home with you—whatever protection is needed.

The hard disk system is far less secure. Anyone with a little knowledge of DOS can easily examine most files on the system and glean whatever knowledge is stored there. Files can be encrypted through some application programs (like *dBASE III Plus* and *Lotus Symphony*), but in most cases the files are easily accessible.

Even erasing a file you have been using gains little protection. Erasing a file changes only one bit in the file directory. If nothing has been written on the disk since the erasure, the former file is still intact on the disk and can be accessed using a simple unerase utility. Unerase utilities change the one bit in the file directory back and checks to be sure the data is still intact.

In some ways a network system is less secure than a single-user hard disk system, and in some ways it is more secure: it depends on how the network is implemented. The servers are the most vulnerable access points to the network. Anyone who can gain access to a server can learn the network names of all resources on the server by simply examining the AUTOEXEC.BAT file. The file will generally not contain passwords, but the NET USE commands in the file describe each private directory and the network access name for that directory. From this information you can log onto the network using any session name (valid or not), and take your choice of network resources using the network names.

The conclusion is simple: if you do not use passwords, the network is open to anyone who has server access. If security is important, keep the server in a secure area. If financial data on the server is the most sensitive data stored, keep the server in the financial department and control access to this department. Lock the server keyboard when it is not being used or unplug and remove the keyboard.

The administrator should recognize that the documentation defining network names and passwords is sensitive information. The storage, copying, and distribution of this information (in a secured environment) should be treated with great caution.

Even in a network with hard disks, you may wish to keep sensitive data on floppy disks so it can be removed and stored in a secured area. For example, you might have a general ledger system program on a hard disk, but the data 'for the program always remains on a floppy disk.

In most cases you will not find it necessary to use passwords. Selecting network names carefully and limiting their distribution should provide enough security. For example, you could use "GXEQBPSZ" as a network name. Remember that a private directory is only private in the sense that the network name for the directory is distributed to a single user. A departmental directory is one in which the network name is distributed through a department. If you do use passwords, these are not stored in the AUTOEXEC.BAT file when you save the configuration, and must be entered each time the network is started. You can edit the AUTOEXEC.BAT file to include the passwords and the file will work properly, but anyone examining the AUTOEXEC.BAT file can see the passwords.

As a final precaution, you may wish to invest in application programs that provide encryption for stored data. For example, the network version of *dBASE III Plus* can encrypt database files and fields of files.

USING APPLICATION PROGRAMS

The administrator has the responsibility of defining programs that will be supported on the network. Many users have their own favorite programs that can be used on the user machines, but you may wish to provide corporate endorsement for certain programs and support these programs on a server machine for use by everyone on the network. If a user chooses to use one of the endorsed programs, they can get help from the server operator or perhaps from a corporate "microcomputer lab" that tests programs for corporate use. If a user decides to choose his or her own software, he or she must use it on the workstation or private directory and he or she can't expect support or tutorials on the program.

As long as users are using different programs on the network at the same time, single-user application programs can often be used on the network with no changes required. This is not always true, however. For example, single-user *dBASE III* will not run from a workstation on a network, even for a single-user. You must have the network version of *dBASE III*. But two users can each use their own version of *Lotus 1-2-3* on their local machines, with separate data files on the private directories of a server machine, with no danger of destroying each other's files or data.

When two or more users are using the same copy of the program or the same data files, you can have serious problems unless the programs are designed to support network use. For example, if two users are using Microsoft *Word* at the same time and it is stored on the public directory of a server machine, you could expect problems (even if they were working with separate documents) unless the Microsoft *Word* version in the public directory supported networking. Many programs create temporary files as they operate, using special names that the user cannot define. If two users are both using the program, you could expect problems with these temporary files.

For this reason, for safety you should always observe the following rule: *When using application software on a network, be sure the software supports a network environment and that you are abiding by any license restrictions imposed by the application software manufacturer.* When purchasing software, be sure it supports your network. Even if you have a single-user system and you plan a network eventually, consider the future by using application software for which networking versions are available.

Beginning with DOS 3.1, Microsoft began to provide tools for software developers in the operating system to support networking. It is still up to the application software designers, however, to take advantage of these functions in their application software. Just because a program is running under DOS 3.1 or later does not mean that it will support networking simply because the operating system supports networking; the application designer actually has to have modified the program to take advantage of the new DOS features.

As an example, let us take *dBASE III Plus* and look at what happens when an application is changed from a single-user environment to a networking environment. Assume that, as a user, we have a single master inventory file and plan several peripheral data files to be used by shipping and receiving. The system began with single-user support. A clerk entered transactions as parts came into the inventory or were shipped. Eventually the work load became too large, and a networking system was installed. The master inventory file remained on the server and several clerks in shipping and receiving use it on several systems.

dBASE III operates with buffers for each data file and index that is in use. Each user is looking at the same data file, but for each user some of each file is in memory and some on the disk. If there were two or more users for any file at the same time, it would not take very long before the file would become very damaged. If the users were only reading files it would work correctly. It is only if two or more people try to update a file at the same time that problems are experienced on the network.

To resolve the problem, application software for networks uses either *file locking* or *record locking*. If file locking is implemented, the network will only permit one person to open the file for writing at a time. If a second person tries to open the same file for writing, the application program returns an error message and may wait patiently for the file to be free. Record locking goes one step further. If record locking is implemented, two people may open the same file for writing, but they cannot write to the same record at the same time. When two people try to write to the same record, the second one to use the record is forced to wait until the first person has completed the task. When an application program is modified for network use, it includes features for file or record locking.

Application programs for networks also often include new features for data security. This is necessary because data files on a network are accessible by others on the network. You may want certain parts of a data file to be available at a departmental level, and other parts to be accessible only to one or two people. For example, with *dBASE III* you may create an employee file that is used by several people on the network. Addresses and telephone numbers in the file may be accessible to anyone on the network, but if salaries or birth dates are included in the same file, you would want this data to be far more secure.

dBASE III Plus includes a separate networking version for a single user on a network. That is, you can install this version on a network and use it from a single workstation. If you are using *dBASE III Plus* on a network with several users, you must purchase additional *LAN Paks*. These permit the support of additional users. This network version provides file locking, record locking, and encryption security for each record at the field level. Even with this, however, you should not take your current application software and run it under the networking version of *dBASE III Plus* and expect it to work efficiently. You must still go into your *dBASE III* programs and modify them to implement the file and record locking that is now supported.

All database management application software is not alike in the way networking is supported. Some do it far better than others. Some include automatic file and record locking, in others you have to modify your single-user programs to use these features. These are questions you must address before making a purchasing decision for database management (or other application software). There is a growing tendency for application program designers to support networks, but the quality and level of this support varies widely.

There is another precaution you should observe in purchasing network versions of application software. Networking versions of DOS application programs can generally be used on any network that supports MS-NET and DOS 3.2 or later. This includes the IBM Token-Ring Network. Some application programs may directly interface with the NETBIOS to gain additional speed. Although the NETBIOS has been standardized by IBM, there is no defined Microsoft NETBIOS standard. Bypassing DOS for networking is somewhat like bypassing DOS and using the ROM directly for the video display—you may get away with it for awhile, but you can be sure to experience problems as network standards evolve.

Chapter 18

Alternative Networks

N OW LET US LOOK AT SOME OF THE COMPETING LOCAL AREA NETWORKS and how they compare with the IBM Token-Ring Network.

In developing the IBM Token-Ring Network, IBM took Microsoft's MS-NET redirector software (which is a resident program network shell for DOS) and modified it for their purpose. MS-NET is an OEM product sold by Microsoft. MS-NET is not an end product for a user, but is intended to be used by other manufacturers to develop their own local area network software. MS-NET is a resident program that provides networking support through the use of commands. IBM added the following features to MS-NET and released it as the *PC Local Area Network* product:

1. The *NET* program with a menu-driven mode.

2. The ability to use the server as a workstation.

3. The Installation Aid with its support for easy installations.

4. The messaging system.

Other manufacturers also use MS-NET or software that emulates MS-NET, developing their own software products that are intended to support their own hardware. For this reason, you could expect many of the competing products to work in ways similar to *PC LAN*. In some cases you can mix hardware and software, but you should use extreme caution.

THE 3COM TOKEN PLUS NETWORK

3Com has been in business since 1979 with over 100,000 users on over 10,000 networks. Their primary market has been the local area network market. Their *Ethernet* gained a wide base of support and evolved from well-developed standards used on larger systems. With the increasing competition from Novell's *Netware* and IBM's Token-Ring Network, 3Com released a new *Token Plus* network that provides a wide base of flexibility and support.

The 3Com *Token Plus* network contains the MS-NET redirector and DOS 3.2 support. For this reason it has a high degree of compatibility with application software. It contains a file server, in contrast to the disk server of the older *Ethernet*.

The hardware uses a logical ring topology and a physical bus topology. This means less cable than the IBM Token-Ring Network and no MAU is required. The cable is twisted-pair, similar to the IBM network cable. Since the token ring standards are used by both IBM and 3Com, you should be able to mix IBM or 3Com hardware in a network. 3Com cables work like the IBM cables, and the adapter cards are also compatible.

The network software is modular in nature. 3Com software works on an IBM Token-Ring hardware, and IBM's *PC LAN* software should work on a 3Com network. You only buy the modules you need, adding features if you need them later. The basic module is called *3+Share*. You can then add any of the various modules as you need them:

3+Mail	Electronic Mail
3+Menu	Menu system
3+Backup	Backup system
3+NetConnect	Connects 3+ to older *Ethernet*
3+3270	Connects 3+ to IBM mainframe

The messaging system is one of the best of any network. *Token Plus* also supports extensive communications gateways, including dial-in access.

Whereas IBM is primarily designed to support IBM equipment, *Token Plus* provides a wide base of support. It will eventually include a bridge to the AppleTalk network. *Token Plus* already provides much more gateway support than the IBM Token-Ring Network.

NOVELL'S NETWARE

Novell's *Netware* has a well-deserved reputation as being the fastest local area network on the market. Benchmark tests often show it two to ten times faster than competing networks. Several versions of the product exist for various types of computers, but the type of most interest to those using the IBM personal computers is the S-Net version of Novell's *Advanced Netware*.

The *Netware* software can also be run on hardware produced by a variety of manufacturers.

Netware obtains its blazing speed by using a special operating system on the server. The operating system simulates DOS with a special shell that transfers data to the server disk using a cache. In a layperson's language, this simply means that disk transfers are minimized by keeping the most recently used parts of a file in memory. No disk transfer is required if a part of the file already used is already in memory.

This special operating system is also the major disadvantage of *Netware*. It is not DOS, and the MS-NET redirector is not used. The server disk format is not a DOS format, which makes it impossible to use programs that require key disks or other special disk formats. DOS application software may or may not work with the *Netware* simulation, and a dealer may have to help you determine if your application software will run on *Netware* and what patches, if any, are necessary.

Another disadvantage is the complexity of the system. There are 71 commands, about three times as many as are used by competing networks. Installation is complex and time-consuming, because the disk must be formatted before the software can be loaded and the network started. Installation requires hours, sometimes days. This is a serious disadvantage if the system goes down and you need to have the network operational again immediately.

If you are willing to live with the disadvantages, you will find the product one of the best in other respects. The Microsoft DOS was never really designed to support networking. If you have a Novell server and DOS on your workstation, and access files through the network on the non-DOS *Netware* server, you will make an interesting discovery. You will find file access through the network (using the Novell operating system) is faster than reading a local DOS file. The messaging system on *Netware* is excellent. The security system on *Netware* is one of the best of any local area network.

The Novell networking shell on a DOS workstation takes only about 23K of memory. This leaves you plenty of free memory for application programs. Unlike *PC Local Area Network,* you have not lost half of the computer's memory to gain networking.

Netware is most efficient used with a dedicated server sold by Novell. You can also use almost any IBM-compatible computer with a hard disk as a server (but the hard disk will have to be reformatted). A dedicated server must have at least 320K of memory. If you wish to use the server as a workstation as well (non-dedicated server), you will need at least 512K of memory. That doesn't leave much room for application programs on the server.

The topology is a star, with a cable between each workstation and the server. You can use multiple servers, connecting them with cables. You will use a lot of cable. Since each workstation has its own cable (channel), no contention scheme is necessary.

THE IBM PC NETWORK

The new IBM Token-Ring Network also competes with IBM's own older PC Network. Both use nearly the same software, although the Token-Ring Network uses an updated version. If users are familiar with the older system, they can use the new system with the same commands.

The hardware, though, is radically different. The PC Network hardware uses the CMSA/CA broadband contention system. As a result, the adapter cards have analog components and the cabling is coax. Like almost all CMSA/CA systems, the network can slow down dramatically or lock up under very heavy loads. The topology is a tree-like structure, and the cabling system is quite complex.

Most vendors are increasingly supporting the token ring topology and switching (as IBM did) to the token ring as quickly as possible. The token ring network is not for everyone, however. You may still wish to use one of the older technologies if you have a small network and plan to keep it small, already have coaxial cable installed, or need the broadband support. In this case the IBM PC Network or the older 3Com system may be just what you need.

Appendix

Appendix A

Controlling
Network Performance

THE SERVERS AND WORKSTATIONS IN A NETWORK CAN BE TUNED WITH various startup parameters to improve performance. These can only be altered when the network is started. To change a value, you must restart the network on the affected system. Some of these can be changed from the startup menu. All of them can be changed using the NET START command. Some affect only a workstation (user), others affect only the server, and some affect both.

ASG:*n*
Maximum Number of Network Devices and Directories

The ASG:*n* parameter defines the maximum network devices and directories that can be used with the NET USE command at one time. The default value is five. The maximum value is 32. Affects user only.

CMD:*n*
Maximum Number of Active NETBIOS Commands

This command, together with the / SES command, controls the way the network uses the adapter. Normally this does not need to be changed. / CMD sets the number of NETBIOS commands that can be active in the network adapter card at one time. The / SES parameter sets the number of sessions that can be active at one time. Increasing this forces the adapter to break the transmissions into more segments of a smaller size. When these values are not specified, they are computed automatically. Affects user and server.

MBl:*n*
Size of Message Buffer

Defines the size, in bytes, of the message buffer used to receive messages. The available range is 512 to approximately 60K bytes; the default value is 1750 bytes. If a message exceeds the buffer size, the excess characters are lost. Affects user and server.

NBC:*n*
Number of Network Buffers

Defines the maximum number of network buffers. The default value is 3. This value should be set to a value greater than the number of files that can be concurrently open on the network. The product of /NBC and /NBS cannot exceed 32K. For sequential processing (such as word processing), you would use a low value. For database applications with many files, use a large value. Affects user only.

Both /NBC and /NBS are the most important parameters for tuning network performance. Changing these can dramatically affect network performance.

NBS:*n*
Size of Network Buffer

Defines the maximum size of the network buffers, and can range from 512 to 32K bytes. The default value is 512. A value of 2K or more is recommended (see /NBC). Larger values will require more memory space in your computer. Affects user.

PBx:*n*
Size of Print Buffer

Defines the maximum size of the print buffer for files sent to the network printer. The value of *x* defines the printer, and *n*, is the buffer size. The value can range from 80 bytes to 16K for one or two printers, less for three or more. The value should be less than or equal to the /RQB parameter of the server that shares the printer to be used. The default value is 1024 bytes. Affects user.

PCx:*n*
Print Count

The value of *n* defines the maximum number of characters sent from the print buffer to the printer in a single operation, with *x* defining the number of the printer (2 = LPT2). This will normally only need to be changed for a faster printer, with typical values for the faster printers ranging from 100 to 200; change in increments of 50 only. The larger the value, the faster the printer will print. The smaller the number, the better the foreground response. If not specified, the /PRB parameter is used as a default. Affects server.

PRB:*n*
Print Buffer

This defines the size of the buffer used to transfer data from the print queue to the printer. The default of *n* value is 512 bytes. The server will require twice the value of PRB in memory space. If you have sufficient memory available, increase this value to 2K. This will reduce disk activity and show noticeable speed improvement with higher-speed printers. Affects server.

PRP:*n*
Printer Priority Control

Defines priority for printing the contents of the background print buffer. The value of *n* can range from 1 (low priority) to 3 (high priority). If the queue backs up, this value should be raised. If the queue stays fairly empty and users can wait for printouts, keep the value low. Affects server.

Like other values, /PRP can only be adjusted at startup. That is a shame, because it often needs to be adjusted dynamically to the current need.

RDR:*n*
Maximum Number of Active Workstations

This defines the maximum number of active workstations that can use a server at one time. The value of *n* can range from 1 to 29, with a default value of 10. Affects server.

REQ:*n*
Server Requests

This parameter defines the number of server requests, *n*, that the server can process at one time. The value can be 1 to 3, with a default value of 2. If the server is dedicated, the value of 1 should not be used. If the server is very busy, try using a value of 3 and an /RQB of 16K. The value of /REQ times /RQB cannot exceed 48K. Affects server.

RQB:*n*
Network Transmission Buffer Size

This is the size of the buffer used for transferring network data to the queue when printing. The default value of *n* is 8K bytes. If server memory is available, you might increase this to 16K to reduce disk activity. Affects server.

SES:*n*
Number of Active Sessions

This parameter sets the number of sessions that can be active at one time (see CMD:n). Affects user and server.

SHB:*n*
Network Buffer Size

Defines the buffer size for network files open for shared use. The default value of *n* is 2K, and can be defined from 512 bytes to 60K bytes. This parameter and the /SHL parameter are only relevant for applications using concurrent updates of shared files, such as database management. Affects server.

SHL:*n*
Number of Active Locked Ranges

When a file is open in a write mode for record sharing, a portion of the file is locked to other users. This defines the maximum number of locked ranges, *n*, that can be used in a file at one time. The value can range from 20 to 1000, and the default value is 20. Each lock uses 14 bytes. Affects server.

SHR:*n*
Maximum Number of Resources Shared

The maximum number of devices that can be shared using the NET SHARE command. The value of *n* can range from 1 to 150, with a default value of 5. Affects server.

SRV:*n*
Maximum Number of Machines Used

Defines the maximum number of different computers that can be used with the NET USE commands at one time. The default value is 2 on a workstation and 3 on a server. The maximum value is 31. Affects user.

TSI:*fb*
Server Time Allocation

The computer processor time is divided between the foreground tasks (the application program) and background tasks (processing network requests and printing). The TSI value controls how this time is divided. The value is a two-digit number. The first digit determines how many timer ticks to allocate for foreground tasks before they are stopped, and the second defines the number of timer ticks for the background tasks before they are stopped. Each time tick is about 54.945 milliseconds. The following table can be used to correlate TSI values to timer ticks:

TSI value	Timer ticks
0	1
1	2
2	3
3	5
4	7
5	11
6	15
7	21
8	28
9	36

The default TSI value is 54, or 5 foreground intervals and 4 background intervals. (This represents 11 timer ticks foreground to 7 background, or 604.395 milliseconds against 384.615 milliseconds.) With a TSI value of 00, background tasks will always have priority and foreground tasks will only run if there are no background tasks (dedicated server).

If there are no background tasks (such as print spooling), try a TSI value of 00. If you are spooling to a printer, try a value of 26.

Some programs that are time-dependent ignore the TSI parameter. For examples, DOS programs such as FORMAT and COPY may block any background activity until completion. Some application programs ignore time slicing. Affects user and server.

USN:*n*
Number of Additional Names

This defines the maximum number of additional names (aliases and forwarding names) that can be used on the computer at one time. The value of *n* can range from 0 to 12, with a default value of 1. Each name requires approximately 600 bytes of storage.

PC LAN
Command Overview

Start the main menu:

   NET

Continue a function:

   NET CONT[INUE] *function*

Continue printing:

   NET CONT[INUE] PRINT[= *printdevice*]

Check network errors:

   NET ERROR [/ D]

Check status of open files:

   NET FILE

Check status of a particular file:

   NET FILE [*d:*] [*path*] *filename*

Close a particular file on your computer:

NET FILE [*d:*] [*path*] *filename* /C

Forward messages to another computer:

NET FOR[WARD] {*sessionname*}

Stop forwarding:

NET FOR[WARD]

Log messages to a file:

NET LOG [*d:*| \ \ *sessionname*] [*path*]*filename*

Log messages to a device:

NET LOG {*printdevice*|CON}

Toggle logging on or off:

NET LOG {/ON | /OFF}

Display log status:

NET LOG

Add an alias name:

NET NAME *addname*

Delete an alias name:

NET NAME *addname* /D

Display name, alias, and forwarding name:

NET NAME

Pause a function:

NET PAUSE *function*

Pause printing:

NET PAUSE PRINT [= *printdevice*]

Pause printing on a remote or local device:

NET PRINT [*d*: | \ *sessionname*] [*path*] *filename printdevice*

Display print status on remote printer:

NET PRINT \ *sessionname*

Display print status:

NET PRINT

Send a message:

NET SEND {*sessionname*|*addname*| * } *message*

Print a separator page defined by filename:

NET SEP[ARATOR] *printdevice* [*d*:] [*path*] *filename*

Print a default separator page:

NET SEP[ARATOR] *printdevice*

Share a directory:

NET SHARE *networkname* = {*d*:] [*path*] *password* | * } {/R | /W | /RW | /WC | /RWC]

Stop sharing a directory:

NET SHARE *networkname* /D

Share a printer:

NET SHARE [*networkname* =] *printdevice* [*password*| *]

Stop sharing a printer:

NET SHARE *printdevice* | *networkname* / D

Display share status:

    NET SHARE

Start the network:

    NET START *configuration sessionname* [*/parameters*]

Start using a directory:

    NET USE *d*: ⟍ ⟍*sessionname* ⟍ {*path* | *networkname*} [*password* | *] directory*

Stop using a directory:

    NET USE *d*: / D

Application Software

THE FOLLOWING SOFTWARE IS ADAPTABLE FOR NETWORK ENVIRONments:

- Database Management:

  DataFlex (Data Access Corp)
  dBASE III Plus (Ashton-Tate)
  Informix-SQL (Relational Database Systems, Inc.)
  R:base 5000 System V (Microrim)
  Revelation (Cosmos)

- Word Processing:

  Microsoft Word (Microsoft)
  Multimate Advantage or *Professional* (Ashton-Tate)
  OfficeWriter (Office Solutions, Inc.)
  Samna Word III and *Samna Word +* (Samna Corporation)
  WordPerfect (Satellite Software International)
  WordStar 2000 and *WordStar Professional Version 4.0* (MicroPro International Corporation)

- Accounting:

  EasyBusiness (Computer Associates)

Medallion (Timberline Systems, Inc.)

Solomon (TLB, Inc.)

(also packages from Real World Corp, Open Systems, Inc., CYMA/McGraw Hill)

The licensing and extra cost for each product to support the networking application must be negotiated with the specific company and can vary. The "standard" version may or may not support networking. Some products may only work with certain types of networks, and the destination network must be specified when purchasing.

Other networking application products are available from a variety of vendors.

Glossary

access unit—(see *multistation access unit*.)
adapter—(see *network adapter card*.)
application software—a computer program designed to serve a particular user function, such as word processing, spreadsheet, database management, etc.
APPS—the public directory on a server hard disk.

baseband system—a networking system in which the channel supports a single digital signal (compare *broadband system*).
batch file—a file of DOS commands used to automate a process on a server or workstation.
broadband system—a networking system in which several analog signals share the same physical network channel (compare *baseband system*).
bus topology—a network geometric arrangement in which a single connecting line is shared by a number of nodes.

carrier—the unmodulated signal used in a broadband network system.
channel—a pathway through which information can be transmitted.
coaxial cable—a type of communications cable consisting of an inner central conductor (usually copper) insulated from an outer conductor that surrounds it.
contention—the method a network uses to determine access to a channel when two or more nodes wish to use it at the same time.

199

CSMA/CD—a contention method (*Carrier Sense, Multiple Access, Collision Detect*) in which a transmitting node first tests the channel and, if the channel is clear, then transmits the desired message. If two stations transmit at the same time, the collision is detected and retransmission is forced.

faceplate—a connecting point in a cable system that permits a network cable from a movable computer to connect with a permanently installed cable system. This is generally a plate installed in the wall.

frame—the basic package of information on a network channel.

Installation Aid—a software program provided with the *PC Local Area Network Program* that can be used to install DOS, configure the necessary directories, install the network software, and install IBM application software on a network server.

link—a communications path between two nodes; a channel.

local area network—LAN; a collection of computers linked so they can exchange information and share resources within a limited geographic area.

logical topology—the geometric arrangement of the nodes and links of a network as they function to support information transfer in the network (see *physical topology, topology*).

log file—a file used on a workstation or server to temporarily store incoming messages.

long-haul services—communication networks (such as the public telephone) that permit computer networking over extended geographic distances.

multistation access unit—a hub in an IBM Token-Ring Network. Each multistation access unit, or MAU, supports up to eight workstations, servers, or combinations. MAUs can be connected to create larger networks.

network adapter card—a card used in IBM-compatible computers to permit their use on a particular type of network.

network name—a name assigned to a server resource to permit it to be accessed and used by a workstation.

node—a connection point in a network for creating, editing, receiving, or transmitting messages.

path—a list of directory names that determines where and in what order DOS will search for a program or batch file.

PC Local Area Network Program—the software component of the IBM Token-Ring Network, also referred to as *PC LAN*.

physical topology—the geometric arrangement of the links and nodes of a network as they physically appear to an observer (see *logical topology, topology*).

prompt—one or more symbols used by the computer to indicate it is ready for data input from a user. The DOS default prompt is the disk drive designator and a right arrow, such as C>.

redirector—that part of the network software that translates a virtual resource request from the user to a real resource on a server.

resident program—a program that remains in memory while other programs are executing. The *PC Local Area Network Program* is a collection of resident programs.

ring topology—a network geometric arrangement in which the nodes are connected point-to-point in an unbroken circular configuration that looks like a ring.

separator page—a page printed on the printer that is used to separate two print jobs. The server operator can define the content of the separator page and whether it is used or not.

server—a system that shares resources with one or more workstations on a network.

session name—a name assigned to a workstation or session to permit it to receive messages or share resources.

star topology—a network geometric arrangement in which all nodes are joined to a central node.

token—a channel access control method in which a token is passed between the nodes on the network; any station with the node at any particular time can then use the network channel (see *contention*).

token-ring—a network system that uses a ring logical topology and a token channel access method (see *contention, logical topology*).

topology—the geometric arrangement of the links and nodes that make up a network. The three basic topologies are the star, ring, and bus.

twisted-pair cable—a type of networking channel cable in which a pair of insulated wires are twisted together. In the Type 1 standard used in the IBM Token-Ring Network, each cable supports two twisted-pair channels (four wires).

virtual resource—a resource (printer, directory, etc.) that is used as if it were on a local workstation, but is actually located on a network server.

workstation—an access point in a local area network for services provided by the network.

Index

3COM Token Plus Network, 182

A
adapter testing, 69
administrator, 170
alias definition, 142
allocation of servers and users, 59
alternative long-haul communication
  services, 6
alternative networks, 181-186
analog signal, 21
APPEND command, 64
application layer, 42
application programs, 178
application software, 197-198
automatic sharing, 113
automatic start, 98

B
backup files, 172
baseband system, 22
batch files, 61, 174
broadband network, 21
buffers, 132, 139
bus topology, 13

C
cable installation, 73
cable planning, 56
cabling, 30, 34, 69

carrier, 21
carrier sense, 23
channel, 11
channel control and access, 20-25,
  20
  comparison of methods of, 25
coaxial cable, 34
collision detect, 23
command line, 97
command mode, 133
communications, introduction to, 20
configurations, 26
connectivity, 7
contention, 23

D
data communications layers, 41, 42
data link layer, 45
data-grade cable, 36
dBASE III PLUS, 8
dedicated server, 29
default settings, 97
digital signal, 21
directories, 75
directory map, 81
directory resources, 120
  sharing of, 107, 112
directory task, 110
disk operating system, 61-68
  starting up, 67

disk redirection (DRDR), 149
disk server, 28
diskette-based workstation, 77
documentation, 74
DOS 3.2, 31

F
fiber optics, 37, 39
file locking, 179
file map, 82
file server, 28
forwarding messages, 143
frame, 24

G
gateways, 30

H
hard-disk workstation, 79
hardware resources, 54
hierarchy, 26
human resources, 58, 170

I
I/O bus alternative, 6
IBM PC Network, 184
IBM Token-Ring Network
  adding non-IBM applications
    programs to, 89
  cable distances for, 57

commands for, 63
detailed analysis of, 53
documentation of, 91
gateways for, 30
hardware for, 27
human factor and, 57
installation of PC LAN software
  for, 77
installation of, 69-91
layer functions in, 45
load factors and, 52
memory requirements of, 55
software for, 30
workstations supported by, 53
inventory control system, 8

J

JOIN command, 64

L

LAN adapter card, 70
  installation and testing of, 71
  setting switches on, 70
  troubleshooting of, 72
law offices, 10
link, 11
load factors, 51
local area networks, 1-10
  advantages and disadvantages of,
    2
  alternative approaches to, 5
  applications of, 7
  cabling of, 34-39, 73
  classification of, 11-25
  components of, 26-33
  defining limits of, 48
  design goals for, 4, 46
  human factor and, 57
  loading of, 51
  management of, 170-180
  multi-user systems vs., 7
  needs of, 49
  planning for, 46-60
  priorities for, 48
  prototype of, 73
  purchase of, 10
  single-user systems vs., 3
  software layers of, 32
log file, 132, 136
logical topology, 17
lost commands, 66

M

mail order system, 10
main installation aid menu, 84
memory requirements, 55
menu alternative, 94
menu mode, 134
menu use, 108
message forwarding, 143

message reception (RCV or MSG),
  150
message system, 131
message task, 135
messenger, 26
messenger wire, 37
modulated analog signal, 22
multiple access, 23
multiprocessor system, 6
multistation access units (MAU), 29,
  70
  connection of, 38

N

names, 75
  additional, 142
  assignation of, 75
net pause, 164
NET SHARE command, 111
NET USE command, 122
NETBIOS, 31
NetWare, 29
network layer, 44
network loading, 51
network names, 76
network performance control codes,
  187-192
network printers
  forcing printing in, 165
  initializing and startup parameters
    for, 160
  management of, 158-169
  net pause use in, 164
  print queue management in, 162
  recovery of, 168
  separator page in, 165
network structures, 11-19
  physical vs. logical topologies in,
    17
network topologies, 11
node, 11
nondedicated server, 29
Novell's NetWare, 182

O

options menu, 85

P

passwords, 115
PATH command, 63
PC LAN program
  command overview for, 193-196
  reconfiguration and startup
    parameters for, 104
  saving configuration of, 100
  server installation of, 79
  starting up, 92-105
  stopping, 104
  using menus of, 103
  withdrawing offers to share, 116

PC Local Area Network (PC LAN),
  26, 31
PCx print count, 162
PERMIT command, 66, 154-157
physical layer, 45
physical topology, 17
polling, 24
PRB print buffer, 161
presentation layer, 42
preventive maintenance, 173
print background program (PRT),
  149
print queue, 162
print redirection (PRDR), 149
print server, 28
print spooling, 28
printer allocation, 113
  automatic sharing in, 114
  command line use in, 113
  menu use for, 113
printers, management of network
  type, 158-169
private subdirectory names, 76
protocols, 40
prototype systems, 73

R

receiver, 26
receiving messages, 136
record locking, 179
redirector, 26
redirector shell, 43
REQ server requests, 160
ring topology, 15
ring-in and -out connector, 38
ROM BIOS, 31
RQB network transmission buffer
  size, 161
rules and conventions, 40-45

S

security, 177
send screen, 134
sending and receiving messages,
  131-146
sending messages, 133
separator codes, 169
separator page, 165
sequential processing, 46
server activity (SRV), 150
server main menu, 99, 109
server operator, 171
server report, 87
server startup, 106-119
servers, 11, 26, 28
  temporary, 153
session layer, 44
session names, 75
sharing resources, 106-119

documentation during, 118
saving configurations for, 119
usting startup parameters for, 118
withdrawal of, 116
Sidekick, 103
sneaker networks, 6
software resources, 56
special networking commands, 147
star topology, 12
star-ring topology, 18
starting and terminating
suspensions, 151
startup batch files, 174
SUBST command, 65
suspending network operation, 147
starting and termination of, 151
Symphony, 62
system integrator, 171

T

telephone networks, 6
temporary servers, 153
token ring, 24
Topview, 78
transaction-based processing, 46
transport layer, 44
TSI server time allocation, 161
twisted pair cable, 35

U

user report, 88
users, 172

V

vendor selection, 59
view screen, function keys for, 140
voice-grade cable, 38

W

wiring closet, 39, 74
word processing, 10
WordStar, 63
workstations, 11, 27
automatic use requests for, 123
NET USE command in, 122
printer resources for, 124
printer use in, 126
saving and printing configurations
of, 130
sharing startup parameters, 129
using menu in, 121
withdrawing offers of use in, 128
workstations, 120-130

Z

zero-slot LAN, 7